The Contemporary Keyboardist™
FOR BEGINNERS

by John Novello

ISBN 0-634-05711-1

HAL•LEONARD®
CORPORATION

7777 W. BLUEMOUND RD. P.O. BOX 13819 MILWAUKEE, WI 53213

In Australia contact:
Hal Leonard Australia Pty. Ltd.

22Taunton Drive P.O. Box 5130
Cheltenham East, 3192 Victoria, Australia
Email: ausadmin@halleonard.com

Visit Hal Leonard Online at
www.halleonard.com

Acknowledgments

I would like to thank my wife Barbara Novello for filling my heart with love; to my parents, John and Menga Novello for their constant unwavering belief in me; to Dwight Mikkelsen for his great copy work of my music examples; to my daughter Rachel Johnson for her great photo; to John Cerullo, Jeff Schroedl, Dan Maske, and staff at Hal Leonard Corporation; to David Miscavige, RTC and the Sea Organization for their support; to L. Ron Hubbard for his absolutely amazing insight into the game of life; and to students of music everywhere whose quest for improvement inspired this work!

Grateful acknowledgement is made to Charlie Banacos for the use of his organizational concepts regarding the nine basic rhythms and chord family breakdowns into chord tones, passing tones, approach tones and tensions. For more regarding Charlie Banacos, go to http://www.charliebanacos.com or contact him at PO Box 272 Manchester, MA 01944

This work is dedicated to beginning students everywhere. I sincerely hope it helps you in your quest to master contemporary keyboard performance.

—*John Novello*

Contents

CD Track List

Audio CD

Track 1: The Five Practice Tools
Track 2: The Musical Alphabet
Track 3: Key Note Locations
Track 4: Half and Whole Steps
Track 5: Sharps and Flats
Track 6: Accidentals
Track 7: Enharmonic Notes
Track 8: Musical Notes
Track 9: Treble and Bass Clefs
Track 10: The Grand Staff with Notes
Track 11: Tied Notes
Track 12: Time Signatures
Track 13: Opus de Dos Notes
Track 14: Walkin'
Track 15: The Perfect Relative Pitch Drill
Track 16: The Five Finger Drill
Track 17: The Key Regimen
Track 18: The Nine Basic Rhythms Drill
Track 19: Free Improvisation 36a
Track 20: Free Improvisation 36b
Track 21: Free Improvisation 36c
Track 22: Free Improvisation 36d
Track 23: Etude #1
Track 24: Reverse Relative Pitch Drill
Track 25: Five Finger Drill for Speed and Endurance
Track 26: C Blues Scale
Track 27: The 12 Blues Scales
Track 28: The Diatonic Major Progression
Track 29: The Basic Rhythm Etude
Track 30: Key Center Improvising
Track 31: Making the Changes
Track 32: The Six Fundamental Basic Chord Breakdowns
Track 33: Etude #2
Track 34: The Five Finger Drill, Rhythm #5
Track 35: The Five Finger Drill, Rhythm #6
Track 36: The Chromatic Scale
Track 37: The Diatonic Progression Circle of Fifths
Track 38: The Tie Drill
Track 39: Etude #3
Track 40: The Triad Drill
Track 41: The Double Thirds Drill
Track 42: The Diatonic Circle of Fifths Voice Led

Introduction

Welcome to *The Contemporary Keyboardist™ for Beginners*. The data you will learn in this course is not necessarily new, but its organization, application and instruction are. All the lesson material is based on what is actually needed to be professional and competitive in the music industry, not on inapplicable theoretical concepts that usually result only in diplomas, certificates, grades, and guess what.... no work 'cause you can't play!—and that's the bottom line. When you play, is it the real McCoy? Can you play songs in different styles? Can you improvise? Can you play the blues? Are you happy with your playing? Can you read and write music if necessary? Can you communicate with feeling when you play and uplift people? Can you sit in and jam with a band? Can you make a living at your profession if you so desire or do you sound like an amateur? If these are your goals, then *The Contemporary Keyboardist™* is for you! It is my belief that all instruction should be structured toward the goals of objective self criticism and self-sufficiency without being forever dependent upon teachers, books, hot licks, etc.

Each lesson is organized in two sections: **Theory** and **Practical**. The **Theory** section will contain the necessary information and instructions along with the intended reason and goal of the lesson. The **Practical** section will contain actual hands-on drills designed to teach you a fundamental musical ability. The audio CD that's included contains recorded versions of all assigned repertoire pieces and examples, so there is no doubt what they should sound like. Make sure, therefore, that you listen to each sound byte as indicated before you begin your practice. At the end of each lesson, there will be an assignment check sheet that you are to do in sequence. When you *honestly* complete each step of the check-sheet, you sign it on the line provided with your initials, including the date you completed it, and move on to the next step. Remember, honesty and integrity are important components of success, so don't check anything off until you have truly mastered it and can play it "effortlessly." It's better in the long run to take as long as it takes to master the assignment, than to glibly skim through it because you're excited to get to the next step. Some of these lessons may take quite a while, but so what! The goal is the ability, not the time it takes!

Even though each lesson is complete unto itself, for additional information on certain topics it is recommended you study the references made to my other works in the **Supplemental Reading** section at the end of each lesson. These materials include the following:

- *The Contemporary Keyboardist™* (Hal Leonard Corp., HL00842012)
- *The Contemporary Keyboardist™, Part 1 – The Basics*: DVD (HL00320555)
- *The Contemporary Keyboardist™, Part 2 – Rhythm, Improv, and Blues*: DVD (HL00320556)
- *The Contemporary Keyboardist™, Part 3 – Working Musician*: video (HL00320192)
- *The Contemporary Keyboardist™, Stylistic Etudes* (HL00842013)

Once the prerequisite lessons are mastered, each lesson in the main course will be divided into six fundamental sections: Ear, Technique, Harmony, Rhythm, Improvisation, and Repertoire. Each fundamental is studied simultaneously in each lesson so the connection is made that they are all interdependent on each other to create real music! In other words, a good ear is necessary to develop good technique and both ear and technique are important to good harmony and improvisation. Also, without a good sense of rhythmic flow, your repertoire (song performance) will suffer completely. Lessons that are to be done in all keys may take a while to complete, and so you shouldn't move on to the next lesson until all keys are mastered. This beginning course concentrates solely on important keyboard and musicianship fundamentals. I also strongly urge you to learn all the etudes in my book *Stylistic Etudes* as this will give you a hands-on application of these fundamentals.

In the end, music is a spiritual communication of your inner soul, and unless you have mastered what you are attempting to play, your inner soul will not achieve "escape velocity" and reach your audience. And last but not least, music is fun, so if you're not having a good time, then you're not playing music!

Yours truly,

—*John Novello*

LESSON 1 • How to Practice

Theory

Practice: The ability necessary to learn the ability! All great musicians, whether formally or self-taught, have at some point spent a considerable amount of time practicing their art form. Practice has to do with study, and study is simply using one's mental faculties to acquire knowledge for the purpose of application. In other words, if you can't apply it (in this case, play your instrument), then you either a) didn't fully master the knowledge you studied, or b) what you studied was not what YOU needed... so keep this in mind.

Model Practice Session

Each practice session, no matter what your level, should consist of the following four parts:

Pre-practice: The period right before actually practicing where you set the goals for the practice session.

Practice: The actual "doingness," where you are trying to achieve a certain ability through repetition, evaluation, attention to detail, reevaluation and comparison to the ideal of what you're trying to achieve.

Post-Practice: The time for reflection on what you intended to accomplish vs. what you actually accomplished, so as to determine the next session's content.

Playing: Simply translated, means playing what *you* want—using whatever abilities and expertise you have developed to date, God-given or otherwise, to express yourself. There is no thinking going on whatsoever, and if there is, then to that degree you are not playing. It is a time to "blow" and have fun, and the best way to end each practice session.

Practice Disciplines

The Five Practice Tools: Track 1 on the CD, "D Minor Funk" on page 8, demonstrates how to use each of the practice tools separately and in combination, so you can eventually conquer any piece.

TRACK 1

1. *Repetition:* Going over and over a section until you have mastered it and can play it effortlessly.

2. *Tempo Variation:* Slowing the section down in order to really learn it. By slowing it down and mastering it at a slow tempo, you can then gradually increase the tempo as long as you master it each time until you attain your final tempo.

3. *Hands Separately:* Practicing a two-handed part with hands separately cuts back the level of difficulty and helps gain confidence for the challenge of the two-handed part.

4. *Phrase Compartmenting:* Isolating a problem area and looping it until effortless mastery is achieved. Apply all other earlier practice techniques.

5. *Outlining:* Playing only the key notes of a passage.

D Minor Funk

Supplemental: Read chapters 1, 2 and 3 in *The Contemporary Keyboardist™*:
Read page 4, *The Basics:* DVD booklet.
View *The Basics:* DVD, the section on practice.

Practical

*

_____ 1. In your own words, describe what a model practice session should consist of.

_____ 2. Define each of the following terms: *pre-practice, practice, post-practice, playing.*

_____ 3. Name the five practice tools by memory and describe how and when they should be used.

_____ 4. Listen over and over to CD Tracks 1–5 to get a good understanding on how to apply each of the five practice tools.

*Remember to initial and date each exercise.

LESSON 2 • Keyboard Familiarization

Theory

Traditional Keyboard Instruments

Dulcimer • This ancestor of the piano originated in Iran shortly after the birth of Christ. It illustrates the basic principles of the piano, hammers striking multiple strings tuned over a flat soundboard. Instead of mechanical hammers, dulcimer players used two light sticks ending with broader blades.

Clavichord • First built around 1400, the clavichord was most popular three centuries later in the music of J.S. Bach. When a key is pressed, a vertical brass strip (tangent) is lifted toward a pair of strings. The clavichord has a quiet tone, but the way it's built allows for some control of dynamics and even vibrato.

Virginal • The typical virginal is a small harpsichord with keys at right angles to a single set of strings. When a key is pressed, a vertical rod (jack) holding a leather or quill plectrum rises and plucks the string, producing a louder tone than the clavichord but without its dynamic variety.

Spinet • Though originating in Italy, the spinet was perfected by English builders in the late 17th century, about the time of composer Henry Purcell. The "jack" mechanism plucks the strings just as in the virginal, but the wing shape permits longer strings, increasing the volume and expanding the range to as much as five octaves.

Harpsichord • Pictured as early as the 15th century, the harpsichord form (where the keys are in line with strings) reached its peak in the period of Bach and Handel. In this shape, the pattern for the modern grand, the strings are longer, and the instrument sounds louder than the clavichord.

Cristofori Pianoforte • In about 1709, Bartolomeo Cristofori built several instruments in the harpsichord shape but with hammer mechanisms surprisingly like the modern piano action. Because players could control soft and loud (piano-forte), which was impossible on plucked keyboard instruments, Cristofori named his new instrument pianoforte!

Piano of Beethoven's Time • During the 18th century, piano builders gradually extended the keyboard. Two important new developments included the escapement action for faster repetition of notes (ca. 1770 by Stein in Augsburg), and the damper and soft pedals (1783 by Broadwood in London). Special pedals, like the ones in this illustration, were often added to produce exotic effects.

Upright Piano • The upright design was already in use for harpsichords in the 16th century. In the 18th century, many builders (especially in Germany) tried to apply this form to the pianoforte. In 1800 the first satisfactory uprights were invented.

 ***Square Grand Piano*** • The square piano originated when German builders (especially Johannes Socher in 1742) tried to adapt Cristofori's pianoforte to the traditional rectangular shape of the clavichord. The square piano was popular until about 1900.

Piano of Lincoln's Time • During the 19th century, the piano continued to become more powerful and responsive. The outstanding improvements were the double-repetition action of Sebastien Erard (Paris, 1821) which allowed very rapid repetition; and the full cast-iron frame of Alphaeus Babcock (Boston 1825), the basis for today's extended keyboard.

 ***Modern Grand Piano*** • The grand piano of today incorporates the best qualities of early keyboard instruments. Cross stringing, a way to achieve greater richness of tone by passing more strings over the center of the soundboard was invented by Alphaeus Babcock in 1830, but was not used in the grand piano until the second half of the 19th century. The sostenuto, or middle pedal, was introduced in the late 19th century, permitting greater musical coloring.

Modern-Day Keyboard Instruments

John Novello's Studio 2B3

In today's fast paced, technologically advanced society, there are many variations of the original piano keyboard and mechanism: organ, electronic piano, synthesizer, disclavier—and when these are connected to a computer through a musical instrument digital interface(MIDI), your imagination is the limit! But whatever keyboard you choose to play, the fundamentals of music and keyboard playing are still the same, so continue studying your fundamentals.

The Piano Topography: The piano keyboard terrain is really one octave with alternating two- and three-key groupings, spread over the entire keyboard.

Example 1: The Piano Keyboard

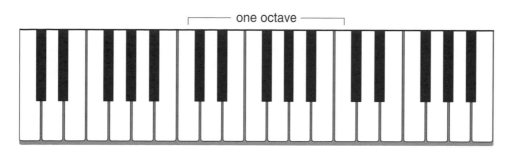

The Musical Alphabet: Unlike the regular English alphabet, the musical alphabet is simply *a b c d e f g*, and then repeats over and over again.

Example 2: The Musical Alphabet

TRACK 2

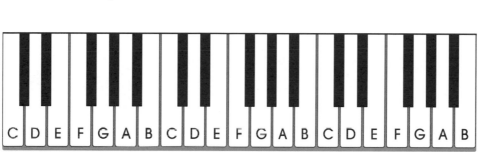

Key Note Locations: Notice for beginning orientation purposes that C is to the left of all the *two* black key groupings and F is to the left of all *three* black key groupings. Also, note that E is to the right of all the *two* black key groups and B is to the right of all the *three* black key groups. This little tip easily locates four of the seven white keys on the piano keyboard which makes locating the other three easy if you know your musical alphabet.

Example 3: Key Note Locations – C and F; E and B.

TRACK 3

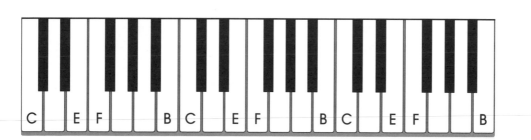

Practical

_____ 1. Go to your keyboard and locate ALL the Cs which are to the left of each two black key group.

_____ 2. Do the same for all the Fs which are to the left of each three black key group.

_____ 3. Do the same for all the Es which are to the right of each two black key group.

_____ 4. Do the same for all the Bs which are to the right of each three black key group.

Supplemental: View *The Basics:* DVD, and booklet pp. 6–7.

LESSON 3 • Accidentals

Theory

Accidentals: An accidental is a mark placed before any of the seven notes of the musical alphabet which indicates that the previously understood pitch of the note should be altered by one or two half steps (semitones).

Important definitions:

Half step: 1) The distance between any two keys (as in E–F or D–E♭) that are next to each other black or white; 2) a musical interval (distance) equivalent to 1/12 of an octave; also called a **semitone**.

TRACK 4

Whole step: 1) The distance between two notes with one key in between (as in D–E or F♯–G♯); 2) a musical interval comprising two half steps; also called a **whole tone**.

Sharp (♯): A symbol that instructs you to raise a note by a half step.

Flat (♭): A symbol that instructs you to lower a note by a half step.

TRACK 5

Natural (♮): A symbol that cancels a flat or a sharp.

To raise the unaltered pitch by one half step, the sharp is used. To lower it by one half step, the flat is used. To raise the pitch by two half steps, a **double sharp** (𝄪) is used. To lower it by two half steps, a **double flat** (♭♭) is used. A **natural** sign (♮) cancels out a previous active sharp or flat.

Example 4: Accidentals

TRACK 6

In the following example, the note D is used to demonstrate flats, sharps, and naturals. This applies of course, to any and all notes.

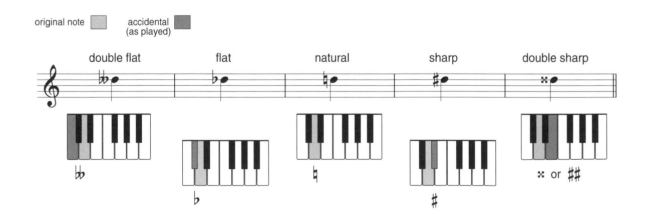

Example 5: Enharmonic Notes

In this next example, all of the black notes on the piano keyboard have two different names or spellings (called **enharmonics**), but sound exactly the same. Even a white key could have two different spellings (i.e., B and C♭ or E♯ and F), but these spellings are rarely used. Which spelling you use is sometimes arbitrary, or a function of what key the music is written in.

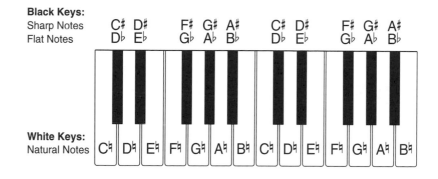

Why do we bother with these symbols? There are twelve pitches that are available. We could give each of those twelve pitches its own name (A, B, C, D, E, F, G, H, I, J, K, and L) and its own line or space on a staff. But that would actually be fairly inefficient, because most music is in a particular key and therefore tends to use only seven notes. So music is easier to read if it has only lines, spaces, and notes for the seven pitches it is (mostly) going to use, plus a way to write the occasional notes that are not in the key. Of the seven note names in the musical alphabet (A, B, C, D, E, F, G), each line or space on the staff will correspond with one of those note names. The twelve pitches are derived from the fact that any of these seven notes can be sharp, flat, or natural. Look at the notes on a keyboard.

Because most of the natural notes are two half steps apart, there are plenty of pitches in between that you can only get by naming them with either a flat or a sharp (on the keyboard, the "black key" notes). For example, the note in between D natural and E natural can be named either D sharp or E flat. These two names look very different on the staff, but they are going to sound exactly the same, since both of them are played by pressing the same black key on the piano.

The following shows D sharp and E flat as enharmonics of each other—two notes sounding the same on the piano, but named and written differently.

Practical

————— 1. Define the following terms: *half step, whole step, sharp, flat, natural, double flat* and *double sharp*.

————— 2. Give three examples of enharmonic note spellings.

————— 3. Using the note B and the various accidentals, write down on the staff below five different ways that B could be named.

————— 4. On the keyboard below, name all the white keys and black keys. On the black keys, give both the sharp and the flat name.

LESSON 4 • The Language of Music

Theory

All subjects have their own language, and music is no exception. The following are the more important symbols and concepts that make up the language of music, and are important to understand before proceeding any further. (For a more comprehensive study, see *The Contemporary Keyboardist*™, Chapter 5, "Symbols and Nomenclature.")

The Staff

The musical **staff** consists of five lines and four spaces. Two staves joined together as in piano notation are called the **grand staff**. We use this staff system to write music.

Example 6: The Staff

Single Staff

Grand Staff

Single staff with musical notes

Bar lines separate the staff into **measures**. A measure is the space between two consecutive bar lines. This organization helps the note-reading process by dividing it into smaller groups which are indicated by a **time signature** (See "Time Signatures," *Example 17*).

As well as the single bar line, you may also meet two other kinds of bar lines. The thin **double bar line** (two thin lines) is used to mark sections within a piece of music. Sometimes, when the double bar line is used to mark the beginning of a new section in the score, a letter or number may be placed above it.

The **final double bar line** (a thin line followed by a thick line) is used to mark the end of a piece of music or of a particular movement within it.

Example 7a: Musical staff with measures and bar lines

In music scores on the grand staff, the upper staff indicates the notes to be played by the right hand, and the lower shows the notes to be played by the left hand. Bar lines are commonly drawn from the top of the upper line on the upper staff to the bottom line on the lower staff. This is illustrated below.

Example 7b: Notes and Bar Lines on the Grand Staff

Musical Notes

Musical tones are represented on a page by characters called **notes**. Notes are visual symbols for sounds created in the physical universe. They tell the performer the pitch (note, i.e., letter-name) and duration (i.e., how long the note will sound).

Example 8: Musical Notes

TRACK 8

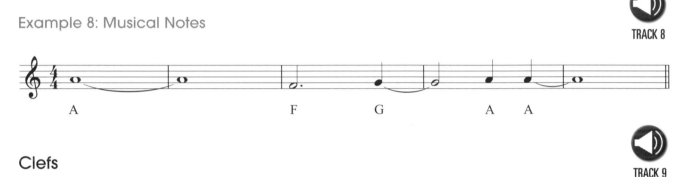

Clefs

TRACK 9

The position of the note on the staff denotes its pitch. A clef sign appearing at the beginning of the staff fixes the pitch of one particular note, and all letter names to follow. The **treble clef** (or G clef) fixes G above middle C and generally applies to the higher notes or frequencies. The **bass clef** (or F clef) fixes F below middle C, and generally refers to lower notes or frequencies.

Example 9a: Treble Clef

Example 9b: Bass Clef

Ledger Lines

Notes that are too high or too low to be placed on the staff appear on short lines below or above the staff called ledger lines. Think of them as extra lines and spaces that extend the staff above and below. The higher the pitch of the note, the higher up the staff it will be placed; in other words, the vertical position of a note determines its pitch.

Example 10: Ledger Lines

Note-Learning Drill

The following can be used to help prepare you for actual sight reading. Look at the treble clef and/or bass clef staves below, and randomly write down some notes on music staff paper, describing to yourself what line or space they are on:

Examples:

D is on the fourth line
C is in the third space
C is two ledger lines above the treble staff
B is in the third space below the bass staff

Then, without looking at your chart, correct any you missed or didn't know, and then locate the notes on the piano. The chart below shows the treble clef and bass clef divided up into line notes and space notes for ease of study. Once you master the treble clef, work on the bass clef line and space notes. Finally, mix them together to practice locating them on the keyboard.

Example 11: Treble Clef Notation

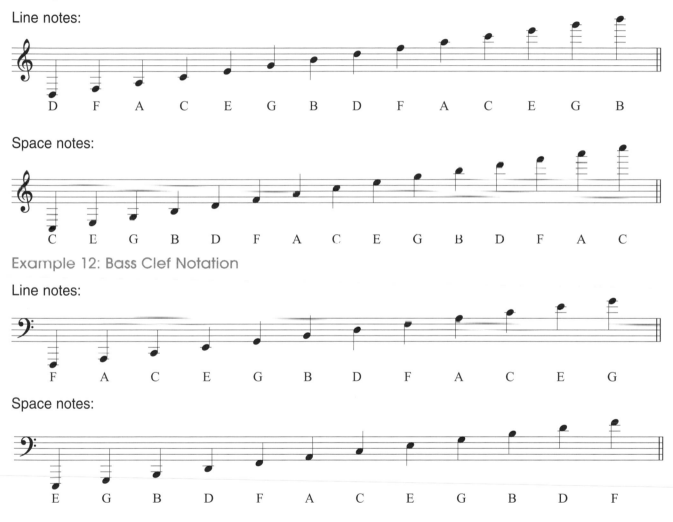

The following grand staff shows the letter names for the lines and spaces on the treble and bass staves. Note that middle C is called middle C because it is the C on the middle ledger line that separates the treble and bass clefs.

Example 13a: The Grand Staff with Letter Names

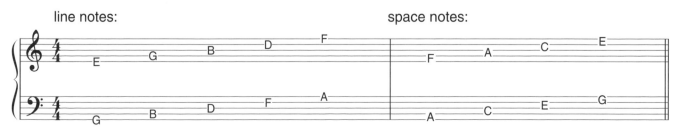

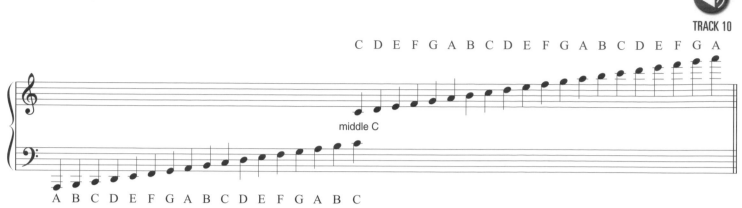

Rhythm notation is a system that defines the time values (durations) of notes and rests (periods of silences). This is done using various symbols. For example, a *note value* is indicated by using the color (white or black) or shape of the *note head*, the presence or absence of a stem, and the presence or absence of flags.

The Parts of a Note

Note duration refers to how long a note is played or sounds. **Rest duration** refers to how long a note is not played or does not sound, i.e., duration of silence.

The simplest-looking note, with no stems or flags, is a whole note. All other note lengths are defined by how long they last compared to a whole note. A note that lasts half as long as a whole note is called a half note. A note that lasts a quarter as long as a whole note is a quarter note. The pattern continues with eighth notes, sixteenth notes, thirty-second notes, sixty-fourth notes, and so on, each type of note being half the length of the previous type. (Note: There are no such things as third notes, sixth notes, tenth notes, etc., but that said, see below to find out how notes of unusual lengths are written.)

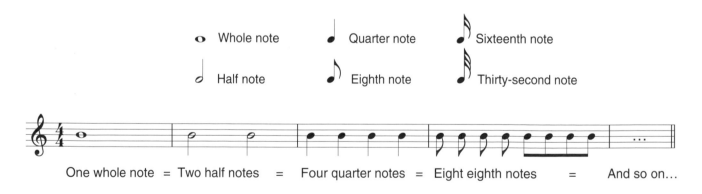

You may have noticed in the figure above that some of the eighth notes don't have flags. Instead, they have a **beam** connecting them to another eighth note. If flagged notes are next to each other, their flags can be replaced by beams that connect the notes into easy-to-read groups. Each note will have the same number of beams as it would have flags.

Beamed Notes

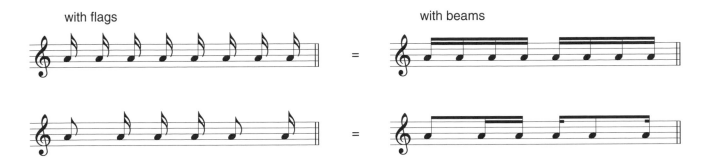

The notes connected with beams are easier to read quickly than the flagged notes. Notice that each note has the same number of beams as it would have flags, even if it is connected to a different type of note. The notes are often (but not always) connected so that each beamed group gets one beat.

Note–Rest Equivalency

Symbol	British Name	American Name	Duration in 4/4 Time	Equivalent Rest
𝅝	Semibreve	Whole note	4 beats	▬
𝅗𝅥	Minim	Half note	2 beats	▬
♩	Crotchet	Quarter note	1 beat	𝄽
♪	Quaver	Eighth note	1/2 beat	𝄾
♬	Semiquaver	Sixteenth note	1/4 beat	𝄿

In written music, standard note lengths are always halves (or halves of halves, and so on) of other note lengths. To get any other note length, dots, ties, or irregular subdivisions must be used. These more complex rhythms will be studied in a later lesson.

Dotted Notes

One way to get different lengths (other than halves of other notes) is by dotting the note or rest. A dotted note is one-and-a-half times the length of the original note without the dot. In other words, the note keeps its original length and adds another half of that original value because of the dot. A dotted half note, for example, would last as long as a half note plus a quarter note, or three quarters of a whole note. A dotted quarter note would be the length of a quarter note plus an eighth note because an eighth is half the length of a quarter note.

Example 14a: Dotted Notes

Dotted whole note	𝅝·	=	𝅝	+	𝅗𝅥		6 counts
Dotted half note	𝅗𝅥·	=	𝅗𝅥	+	𝅘𝅥		3 counts
Dotted quarter note	𝅘𝅥·	=	𝅘𝅥	+	𝅘𝅥𝅮		1 1/2 counts
Dotted eighth note	𝅘𝅥𝅮·	=	𝅘𝅥𝅮	+	𝅘𝅥𝅯		3/4 count
Dotted sixteenth note	𝅘𝅥𝅯·	=	𝅘𝅥𝅯	+	𝅘𝅥𝅰		3/8 count

The following chart shows both standard and dotted-note values in descending order of magnitude, as well as some of the ways that they appear: stems up, stems down, beamed together, etc.

Example 14b: Note Duration Table

Note Name	Notation	Count in 4/4 Time
Whole note	𝅝	4 counts
Dotted half note	𝅗𝅥·	3 counts
Half note	𝅗𝅥	2 counts
Dotted quarter note	𝅘𝅥·	1 1/2 counts
Quarter note	𝅘𝅥	1 count
Dotted eighth note	𝅘𝅥𝅮·	3/4 count
Eighth note	𝅘𝅥𝅮	1/2 count
Dotted sixteenth note	𝅘𝅥𝅯·	3/8 count
Sixteenth note	𝅘𝅥𝅯	1/4 count
32nd note	𝅘𝅥𝅰	1/8 count

Multiple Dots: A double dot adds 1 3/4 times a note's basic value. A triple dot adds 1 7/8 times a note's basic value and is extremely rare. (See "Prelude in G Major" by Frédéric Chopin.) Although dotted rests aren't used as much as dotted notes, the table shows the common rests in descending order of magnitude.

Rests

Just as notes have duration, so does silence, or rests. Rests are used to indicate that no notes are to be played for the period of time defined by the particular rest notated. For example, a quarter rest indicates you should not play anything for one count. As with note notation, a dot immediately after a rest indicates you lengthen the rest by one half of the rest's value.

A rest stands for a silence in music. For each kind of note, there is a written rest of the same length. The most common rests are as follows:

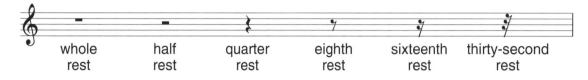

| whole rest | half rest | quarter rest | eighth rest | sixteenth rest | thirty-second rest |

Example 15: Rest Duration Table

Rest Name	Notation	Counts
Dotted whole	▬.	6 counts
Whole note	▬	4 counts
Dotted half	▬ .	3 counts
Half	▬	2 counts
Dotted quarter	𝄽·	1 1/2 count
Quarter	𝄽	1 count
Dotted eighth	𝄾·	3/4 count
Eighth	𝄾	1/2 count
Dotted sixteenth	𝄿·	3/8 count
Sixteenth	𝄿	1/4 count

Tied Notes: Yet another way to extend the value of a sound or note is through the use of a tie—a curved line that connects notes of the same pitch which extend the value of the first note for the full value of both notes. The second note (or tied note) is not played again.

Example 16: Tied Notes

Time Signature: This sign is placed on a staff to indicate the meter, commonly a numerical fraction. The numerator shows the number of beats per measure and the denominator represents the kind of note (half, quarter, or eighth note) getting one beat. Example 17 shows some commonly used time signatures.

Example 17: Time Signatures

TRACK 12

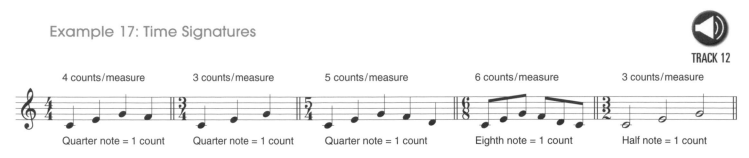

Special Time Signatures: Common Time and Cut Time

In earlier times it was common practice to only indicate the number of beats in a bar. Triple meter (3/4) or *tempus perfectum* was represented by a circle (according to Pythagoras the sphere represents perfection), while *tempus imperfectus.* (4/4) was represented by a half circle in the form of a letter C. Duple meter (2/2) was represented by a semicircle with a vertical line. The two latter symbols have remained in use even if they now appear in a somewhat stylized form.

The first symbol is called **common time**, representing four quarter-note beats in a measure. The second symbol, similar to the first, but crossed with a vertical line, is called *alla breve* (Italian, literally "according to the breve") or **cut time**. It represents two half-note beats in a measure.

Example 18: Common and Cut Time

Cut time, as used in dance music or jazz generally means that the music is played twice as fast as you would ordinarily expect, based on the notes. Where normally a quarter note would correspond to a beat, now the half note becomes the unit of counting.

In summary, many different kinds of symbols can appear on, above, and below the staff to communicate the musician's language. The notes and rests are the actual written music. Other symbols on the staff, like the clef symbol, the key signature, and the time signature, tell you important information about the notes and measures. Symbols that appear above and below the music may tell you how fast it goes (tempo markings), how loud it should be (dynamic markings), what the harmony is (chord symbols), and even give directions for how to perform particular notes (accents and phrase markings). Example 19 is a short piece of music with many of the common music symbols labeled for your understanding.

Supplemental: For a more comprehensive look, see *The Contemporary Keyboardist*™, Chapter 5, "Symbols and Nomenclature."

Opus de Dos Notes

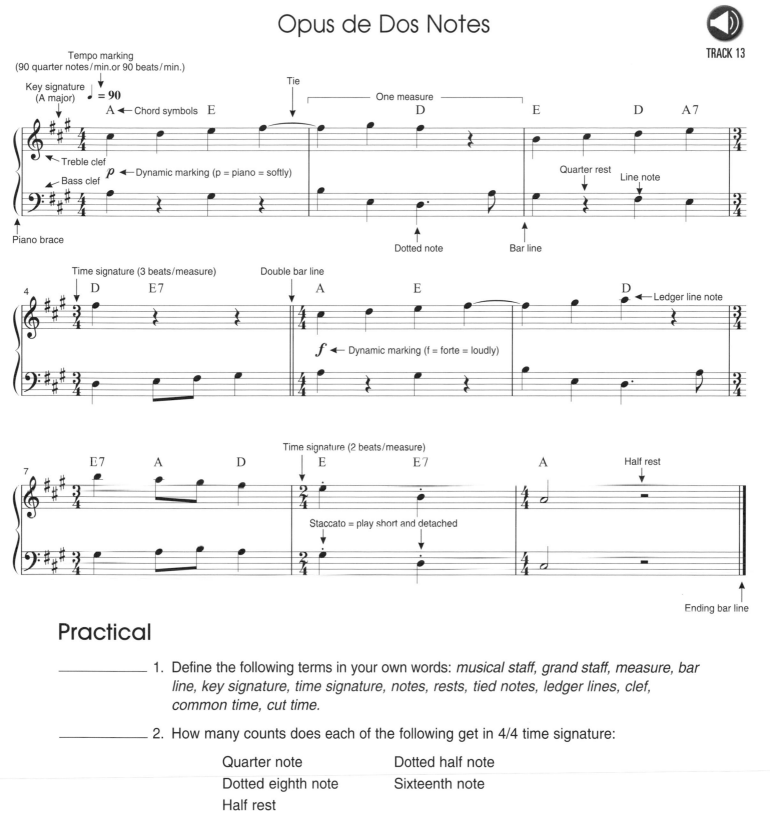

Practical

_____ 1. Define the following terms in your own words: *musical staff, grand staff, measure, bar line, key signature, time signature, notes, rests, tied notes, ledger lines, clef, common time, cut time.*

_____ 2. How many counts does each of the following get in 4/4 time signature:

Quarter note	Dotted half note
Dotted eighth note	Sixteenth note
Half rest	

_____ 3. Name the following notes and locate them on your keyboard:

_____ 4. In the following piece of music, identify all musical symbols you have studied so far.

Walkin'

TRACK 14

LESSON 5 • Key Signatures

Theory

The concept of tonality came into being during the Renaissance period, and was established during the Baroque period. It continued into the Classical and Romantic periods, and onward to today's modern music—jazz, pop, blues, rock, rhythm and blues, country, etc. Tonality is related to the use of major and minor scales.

When a piece is built on a major or minor scale, the root or tonic of this scale acts as the tonal center, which means the piece revolves around this note and is considered to be in the tonality or key related to this scale. For instance, if the scale is a major scale of D, the key is D major, which means that most of the melody and chords are derived from or based on the D major scale.

The **key signature** is located at the beginning of a musical staff, and graphically lists which notes are to be played sharp or flat, thereby determining the key of the piece. It is positioned right after the clef symbol on the staff, and may have either some sharp symbols or flat symbols on particular lines or spaces. If there are no flats or sharps listed after the clef symbol, then the key signature is "all notes are natural," unless a specific note has an accidental in front of it within the music.

In standard notation, clef and key signature are the only symbols that must appear on every staff. They appear so often because they are such important symbols. The clef tells you the letter names of each line and space note on the staff (A, B, C, etc.), and the key tells you whether the note is sharp, flat, or natural.

Example 20: Relationship of Clef, Key Signature, and Notes

On this treble clef staff:

On this bass clef staff:

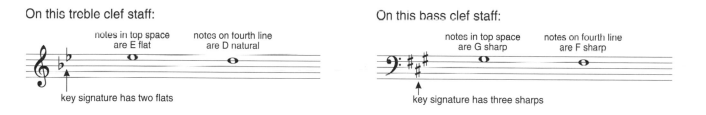

When a sharp or flat appears on a line or space in the key signature, all the notes on that line or space are sharp (or flat), and all other notes with the same letter names in other octaves are also sharp or flat.

Example 21: Key Signature Translation

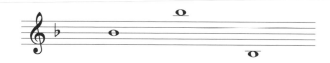

This key signature has a flat on the "B" line, so all of these Bs above are flat. The sharps or flats always appear in the same order and position in all key signatures. This is the same order in which they are added as keys get sharper or flatter. For example, if a key (G major or E minor) has only one sharp, it will be F sharp, so F sharp is always the first sharp listed in a sharp key signature. The keys that have two sharps (D major and B minor) have F sharp and C sharp, so C sharp is always the second sharp in a key signature, and so on. The order of sharps is: FCGDAEB. The order of flats is the reverse of the order of sharps: BEADGCF. So the keys with only one flat (F major and D minor)

have a B flat; the keys with two flats (B flat major and G minor) have B flat and E flat; and so on. The order of flats and sharps, like the order of the keys themselves, follows a circle of fifths. (See Example 25).

Example 22: Order of Accidentals

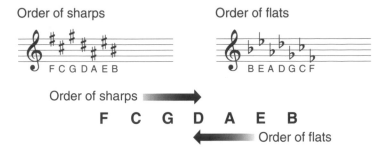

In tonal music, when someone says a particular song is in the key of "X," key is meant as the *main* key of the piece. However, numerous modulations (momentary changes of keys) may occur throughout the music. So if this is the case, having a key signature at the beginning serves the purpose of a) letting the performer know that the piece is based on the key F♯ (utilizing the notes in the F♯ major scale) and b) saves the composer and the reader the headache of writing and reading all the sharps during the song because the key signature takes care of all of this in advance. Notice that the major scale and its relative or natural minor (the same notes of the major scale starting on the sixth degree, e.g., C D E F G A B C = major scale; A B C D E F G A = natural, or relative minor scale) both share the same key signature. What then is the difference you ask? Well, the difference is that the root or tonic in the major is C and in the relative minor is A, so the melody tends to resolve and focus more on that respective tonic.

Examples 23 and 24 are complete key signature tables of all sharp and flat keys for your reference. You should eventually memorize and know these cold! Notice that C♯ has seven sharps, whereas its enharmonic spelling, D♭, has only five flats. Usually, the enharmonic spelling of the key with the least number of accidentals is used. For example, the key of D♭ is used more often than C♯ and B is used more often than C♭—it is normally easier to read the key with less accidentals.

Number of Accidentals	Keys	Order of Accidentals	Key Signature
0 sharps	C major A minor	Not applicable	
1 sharp	G major E minor	F	
2 sharps	D major B minor	F, C	
3 sharps	A major F# minor	F, C, G	
4 sharps	E major C# minor	F, C, G, D	
5 sharps	B major G# minor	F, C, G, D, A	
6 sharps	F# major D# minor	F, C, G, D, A, E	
7 sharps	C# major A# minor	F, C, G, D, A, E, B	

Number of Accidentals	Keys	Order of Accidentals	Key Signature
0 flats	C major A minor	Not applicable	
1 flat	F major D minor	B	
2 flats	B♭ major G minor	B, E	
3 flats	E♭ major C minor	B, E, A	
4 flats	A♭ major F minor	B, E, A, D	
5 flats	D♭ major B♭ minor	B, E, A, D, G	
6 flats	G♭ major E♭ minor	B, E, A, D, G, C	
7 flats	C♭ major A♭ minor	B, E, A, D, G, C, F	

The Circle of Fifths Key Signature Chart

This chart is a shorthand way of remembering the relationship between the key and the key signature. Notice that if one begins at the 12 noon position of a clock and goes clockwise in intervals of fifths upwards: C, G, D, A, E, B, F♯, C♯, you will get all the sharp keys. The *key signature* for each *key* has one sharp more than the key preceding it in the sequence. If one begins at the 12 noon position of a clock and goes counterclockwise in intervals of fifths downward: C, F, B♭, E♭, A♭, D♭, G♭ and C♭, you will get all the flat keys. The key signature for each key has one flat more than the key preceding it in the sequence.

Summary: Picturing a circle of fifths can help you identify key signatures, find related keys, and remember the order of sharps and flats in key signatures.

Example 25: Circle of Fifths

In the following chart, major keys are upper case, and minor keys are lower case.

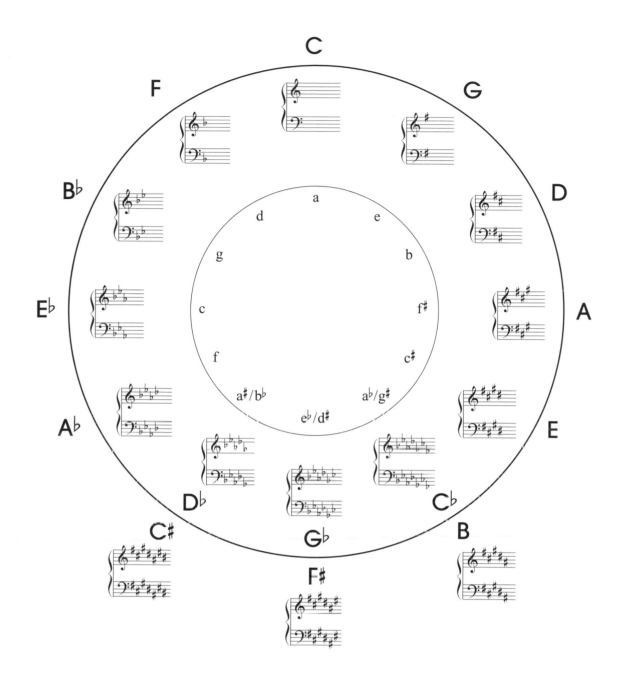

Supplemental: See *The Contemporary Keyboardistt*™, pp. 42–43 for more on the circle of fifths key signature chart.

Practical

_____ 1. Define *key signature* in your own words.

_____ 2. What does it mean when someone says that a particular song is in the key of B♭ in regards to the sharp keys? Flat keys?

3. Name the major and relative minor keys that have the following number of sharps or flats. Write their respective key signatures in the correct positions.

4 flats	7 sharps	No flats No sharps	3 sharps	2 flats
2 sharps	6 sharps	7 flats	1 sharp	1 flat
6 flats	3 flats	5 sharps	5 flats	3 sharps
2 sharps	4 flats	7 flats	1 sharp	6 flats
3 flats	3 sharps	1 flats	5 sharps	No flats No sharps
3 sharps	6 sharps	2 flats	7 sharps	5 flats

4. Name the keys that the following key signatures represent. Include both the major and minor key for each.

5. The key of F has one flat B♭. This means that all Bs on the B♭ line, the third line in treble clef, are flat but not any other Bs. True or False?

6. Draw out the entire circle of fifths, including all major and minor key signatures and their respective number of sharps and flats.

7. Why do key signatures even exist at all? Wouldn't it be easier and more efficient to simply put the flat or sharp in front of the note in the song?

8. Why do the major and relative minor keys have the same key signature?

LESSON 6 • Intervals

Theory

An **interval** is the distance between any two notes. There are two types of intervals: *harmonic*, in which tones are sounded simultaneously and *melodic*, in which tones are sounded consecutively.

Example 26: Intervals

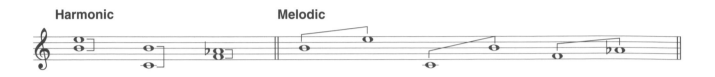

The classification of intervals is as follows:

Simple intervals: Intervals where the distance between the two notes is less than an octave apart.

Compound intervals: Intervals where the distance between the two notes is greater than an octave. Compound intervals can be reduced to simple intervals by subtracting the octave (7 notes) from them. For example, a major 10th reduces to a major 3rd (10 − 7 = 3); a perfect 11th reduces to a perfect 4th (11 − 7 = 4); a major 13th reduces to a major 6th (13 − 7 = 6).

Example 27: Simple and Compound Intervals

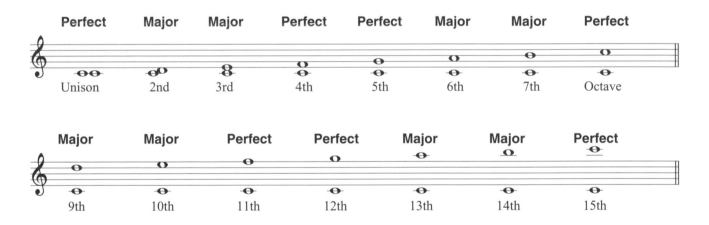

Altered intervals: Intervals whose top notes are lowered or raised by a half step. The following rules are important to use as they will help clarify how chords are constructed later.

Altered Interval Rules:

1. Major intervals made a half tone smaller become minor.

2. Minor intervals made a half tone larger become major.

3. Major and perfect intervals made a half tone larger become augmented.

4. Minor and perfect intervals made a half tone smaller become diminished.

Example 28: Altered Intervals

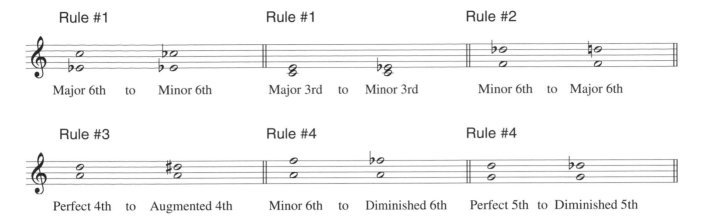

Rule #1	Rule #1	Rule #2
Major 6th to Minor 6th	Major 3rd to Minor 3rd	Minor 6th to Major 6th

Rule #3	Rule #4	Rule #4
Perfect 4th to Augmented 4th	Minor 6th to Diminished 6th	Perfect 5th to Diminished 5th

Enharmonic Intervals: Just as there are enharmonic notes, those that are spelled differently but sound the same, there are enharmonic intervals—intervals that are spelled differently but sound the same.

Example 29: Enharmonic Intervals

Perfect 5th   Diminished 6th   Minor 7th   Augmented 6th   Augmented 2nd   Minor 3rd

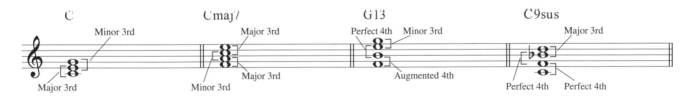

In conclusion, intervals are the basic building blocks of all melodies and chords. A chord is really a combination of two or more intervals as shown in the next example.

Supplemental: See *The Contemporary Keyboardist*™, pp. 56–62 for more on intervals.

Example 30: Chords

C   Cmaj7   G13   C9sus

Supplemental: See *The Contemporary Keyboardist*™, pp. 63–72.

Practical

_____ 1. What is the difference between harmonic and melodic intervals?

_____ 2. What is the difference between simple and compound intervals?

_____ 3. Convert the following compound intervals into simple ones: major 13th, major 9th, sharp 11th, major 10th, major 15th, flat 9th, perfect 12th.

_____ 4. Using the rules for altered intervals, name the following intervals:

Example 31: Interval Naming

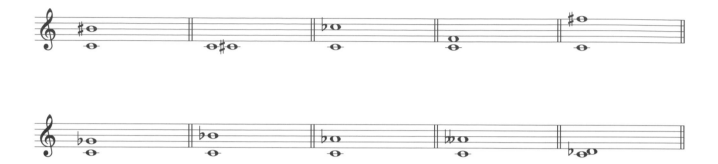

Orientation

Each lesson in the Main Course (Part 2) consists of six fundamental areas: **Ear Training**, **Technique**, **Harmony**, **Rhythm**, **Improvisation**, and **Repertoire**. You are to cover a little of each section at each practice session, so budget your time accordingly. It serves you no constructive purpose to stay on one section for the full practice session as then the rest suffer. For example, if you have an hour to practice, then budget ten minutes or so for each section. It would be best to allocate at least an hour and a half for a productive session. Since it's important to have a full understanding of each of these fundamentals (basics) as they relate to your training and progress, let's take a look at each separately.

First of all, what is a fundamental? A fundamental is a basic! It is one of the minimum constituents without which a thing or system would not be. In other words, to really have a mastery of playing music (the thing or system in this case), then one would have to have a command of the six basics mentioned above. Now whether this command is obtained through self-study or formal study doesn't matter; what does matter is that one understands and applies these basics and thus demonstrably plays and improvises music.

Fundamentals

Ear Training: The goal of ear training is to enable you to simultaneously identify, differentiate, and process certain levels of musical information (melody, harmony and rhythm), resulting in the composite skills and actions of performance. The ear is both receptive and directive. It receives sound images from within (the creative faculties of the imagination) and actual sounds from instruments without. With this data the ear directs the entire performance cycle which includes spirit-mind-body-instrument-audience and vice versa! All the drills and exercises in this area are designed for two reasons: 1) to get the student to accurately play what he hears and 2) to increase what he/she hears. It would be no great accomplishment if we achieved number one, for example, and all the student heard and could play was "Mary Had a Little Lamb"! We would still work on number two so we could increase and improve on *what* the student hears. Now, playing what you hear is everything? But what does this really mean? It means that *you* are hearing in your head, your mind, or whatever you want to call it, what you are playing, either just before you play it, or simultaneously. In other words, you are not just mechanically or logically playing notes that you know work or that *should* work. You are hearing and feeling with certainty and passion what you are playing. You are doing what you are doing when you are doing it and *nothing* else! You are not thinking, wondering, or hoping, but are simply playing what you hear and that's what a musician does!

Supplemental: View *The Basics:* DVD, the section on practice, as well as the DVD *Booklet #1*, pp. 35–36; also see *The Contemporary Keyboardist™*, pp. 123–143.

Technique: To put it very simply, you need the physical coordination to operate the keys and pedals of the piano or keyboard in order to competently play what you hear. Nothing can be more frustrating than to hear some great music in your head and then not be able to play it because you don't have a good effortless technique (chops). That's the opposite extreme of having great technique but not playing what you hear, or playing mechanically with no feel. The exercises and drills in this section are designed to increase your ear-mind-body-piano independence and coordination. Remember, technique is only a tool. You need as much as is necessary to express yourself. The more you have, the more headroom you have and thus the more potential to play effortlessly and express yourself fully.

Supplemental: View *The Basics:* DVD, "Technique," as well as the booklet, page 15. Also see *The Contemporary Keyboardist™*, pp. 371–378.

Harmony: The structure and function of chords (three or more notes played simultaneously) and their relationship to each other. The contemporary keyboardist needs to have a thorough practical knowledge of all chords and their inversions in order to improvise and play musical styles.

Supplemental: See *The Basics:* DVD booklet, pp. 28–34.

Rhythm: The organization of music with respect to time. It holds first place as the basic expressive factor in creating and playing music. A metronome can put out a good click but it can't groove. That's your job! You are responsible for the pocket that makes people "feel" the music.

Supplemental: See *The Contemporary Keyboardist*™, pp. 25–26 and the DVD booklet, *Rhythm, Improv, and the Blues,* pp. 4–11.

Improvisation: My favorite basic! The ability to freely create music is as native to a musician as flying is to a bird. I can't tell you the "musicians" I run into that can't improvise, especially in the classical world. This is simply not okay and is only due to faulty instruction in the basics of music. Improvisation simply means to invent; to compose or recite without preparation; to make or provide from available materials. Any musician should therefore be able to jam with other musicians in any style and freely and effortlessly create!

Repertoire: Repertoire is a list of musical material that you know and can play. How many musicians run into the situation of having to play at some function and don't know any songs. This is preposterous! You should know tons of songs and have them committed to memory… after all you are a musician!

At the end of each lesson there will be a song or study for you to learn. Make sure you listen to the CD rendition and then practice hands separately and together. You should commit each tune to memory. Improving memory is similar to exercising your muscles—they both get better with exercise. If you begin memorizing songs now, soon you will be able to commit hundreds of songs to memory. To memorize a song, simply play it over and over again until your inner ear knows it cold. It will then magically play the song for you, at least that's what it "feels" like. But like anything, you need to build up confidence.

The goal of *The Contemporary Keyboardist*™ *for Beginners* is to help shape a musician who can play what he/she hears, knows all basic chords and inversions, has a good pocket and rhythmic independence, can improvise and jam with other musicians at a basic level, and has a good beginning stylistic repertoire. Let's get started!

LESSON 7 • Getting Started!

Theory

Ear Training

Definitions:

Absolute or Perfect Pitch : The ability to determine a note from its frequency or rate of vibration alone, along with the ability to sing or name a note asked for.

Perfect Relative Pitch: Given a note, the ability to identify any other note. This is done by being able to hold a key center and identify intervals.

TRACK 15

The Perfect Relative Pitch Drill

Mock up the pitch center of C by playing it on the piano until you can sing it, as well as "hear" it in your mind's ear. Then, either by closing your eyes or turning your back to the piano, hit any note, preferably in your vocal range for now (later we do it full range) with the eraser end of a long pencil. By comparing the just struck note with the note C, which should still be in your mind's ear, you will eventually be able to identify the interval, i.e., a fifth or fourth, etc., and thus the note. Your answer should occur in about two seconds as we're trying to develop your intuition not your ability to figure it out using other famous melodic intervals or by cheating and singing up the scale, etc. For now, just strike the white keys until you can identify them easily. This drill is not a one week assignment so don't get down on yourself—it could take quite some time.

Technique

The Five Finger Drill

The purpose of this drill is to develop the coordination of your entire playing mechanism which includes the torso, shoulder, arm, wrist, and fingers. It is called the "five finger drill" because it concentrates on improving your five finger articulation without adding thumb crossing as in scales, which we will practice later. Notice the pattern which is based on C major, C minor, and C diminished. This exercise is to be played in the following manner:

1. Hands separately, MM = 112, two notes per beat, two times through each pattern.

2. Hands together, MM = 112, two notes per beat, two times through each pattern.

Example 32: The Five Finger Drill

TRACK 16

Harmony

The Key Regimen Drill

The *key regimen* is a systematic way of acquiring facility and flexibility in all keys. This is important for improvisation, transposition, and song writing. The following example is written out in the key of C, and includes the first three steps of five. It should be learned first in the key of C, and then over time, in all keys, one key at a time until all three steps are mastered. Fingerings for the right hand are above the staff, and L.H. fingerings are below. (See Appendix A for complete major scales and fingerings.)

Example 33: The Key Regimen

TRACK 17

Step 1) C major scale, two octaves, play hands separately and together.

Step 2) Play six basic triads and their inversions, hands separately and together.

Step 3) Play six basic tetrads and their inversions, hands separately and together.

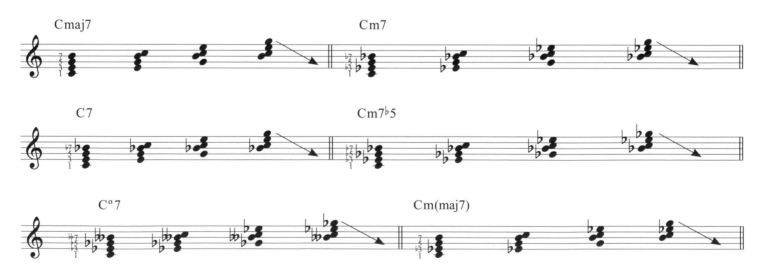

Note: The 7th and 6th can be interchangeable, so Cmaj7 can be changed to Cmaj6, and Cmin(maj7) can be changed to Cmin6. This interchangeability means that Cmaj7 and C6 can substitute for each other in a chord progression. It's just a matter of taste—which one a player or songwriter wants to use.

Example 34: Major 7 and Major 6 Interchangeability

Cmaj7 ←— interchanges with —→ C6　　　　　Cm(maj7) ←— interchanges with —→ Cm6

Rhythm

The Nine Basic Rhythms Drill

The purpose of this drill is to learn how a beat can be subdivided into 2s, 3s, and 4s. It can also help you to develop a good time feel and independence as, after all, "it don't mean a 'thang' if it ain't got that swing!" A beat can be divided into many subdivisions. The following nine are the most basic and thus the most used.

Procedure: Left hand plays quarter notes while the right hand plays the indicated rhythm. Initially, count each rhythm out loud so you can be sure you fully understand each subdivision. Use a metronome setting of a quarter note = 72. Please note that there are really only four unique subdivisions—rhythms 1–4. Rhythms 5–9 are variations of rhythm 4.

TRACK 18

Example 35: The Nine Basic Rhythms Drill

Improvisation

Definition: 1) to compose, recite, play, or sing extemporaneously; 2) to make, invent, or arrange offhand; 3) to fabricate out of what is conveniently on hand. This is the true ultimate goal for a musician—to be able to freely and effortlessly create spontaneous music with his/her instrument and his available resources. Even a beginner can improvise with the "resources" that he or she has on hand if this definition is applied correctly. As one develops more musical abilities, improvisation abilities become more advanced. It's a fallacy that one can only improvise when one is finally a master. As far as what styles one improvises in, well… that's your choice. To be well rounded though, I suggest you expose yourself to many styles of music.

There are three levels of improvisation with regards to music: melodic, harmonic, and rhythmic. During any complete keyboard improvisation, beginning or advanced, all three elements should come into play. Should one's playing lack any of these elements, it doesn't mean it is not an improvisation. However, as one is improvisin,g focus could be placed on only one of these levels (or each one separately) for practice sake.

The following short pieces were *improvs* that I did off-hand with no attention in advance as to style, tonality, complexity, or whatever. I just began extemporizing! Listen to CD Track 19 and watch the music for best results. Then you try creating some music—anything at all is a pass! The only way you can flunk this drill is to not play anything and even that would be considered an improvisation if that's what your improv was—silence for 30 seconds! Too late, if you're thinking of doing this; the late avant-garde composer John Cage did this in the late '40s! His piece was called "4'33"," which stands for "Four Minutes and 33 Seconds." It was performed by David Tudor on August 29, 1952, at Woodstock, New York as part of a recital of contemporary piano music. John was trying to prove a point in that, even though the performer did not play anything at all for four minutes and thirty-three seconds, there was still sound present at the performance due to the surrounding environment.

Example 36: Free Improvisation

TRACK 19

TRACK 20

TRACK 21

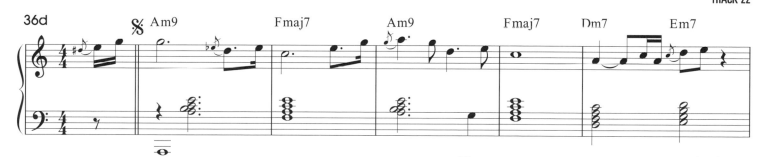

TRACK 22

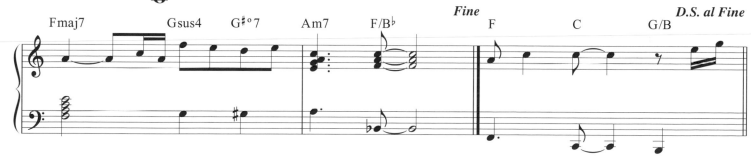

Repertoire

Listen to and learn the following etude (study). For even better results, transpose this song study to all keys.

Etude #1

TRACK 23

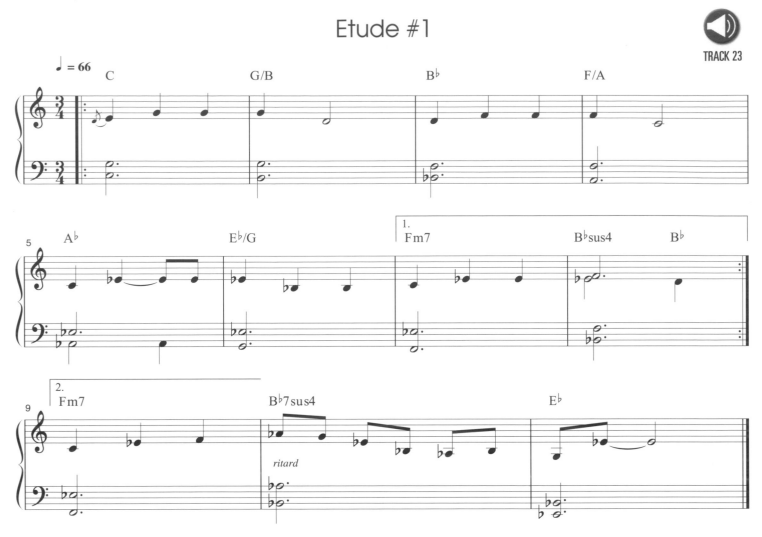

Practical

_____ 1. What is the difference between perfect pitch and absolute pitch?

_____ 2. Reverse roles now in the Nine Basic Rhythms Drill by playing quarter notes with your right hand and have your left hand play each of the nine basic rhythms.

_____ 3. Define musical improvisation.

_____ 4. True or false? One can only improvise once one fully masters all musical rudiments.

_____ 5. What are the three parameters that can be varied while improvising musically?

_____ 6. Sit at the keyboard and without any forethought improvise a song. Do not think about this at all as to length, style, complexity or whatever. When you can do this at will without evaluating the results and have done several songs, then you get a pass!

LESSON 8 • Jazzin' and Bluesin'

Theory

Ear Training

TRACK 24

Perfect Relative Pitch Drill

Continue your drilling of the perfect relative pitch drill but add the black keys. To do this, make sure your pencil is pushed a little more towards the back of the keys so a black key is a possibility. The rest of the procedure is the same.

Reverse Relative Pitch Drill

Given any pitch, be able to sing any other pitch above or below, in your vocal range. It's called "reverse" because instead of guessing the note, you are required to sing the note on command. Figure out your vocal range first, meaning your lowest singable note to your highest singable note. Then, starting with C as your home base, point to any note within your vocal range without sounding it and then just guess at singing it. Do not cheat and sing up a scale or favorite melody to get the answer. Just see if you "hear" the note in your mind and go for it. If you don't, just take a stab at it. If you miss it, play it and then re-sing it for practice.

Technique

TRACK 25

Five Finger Drill for Speed and Endurance

Continue with your five finger drill from page 37, but now start playing four notes per beat at around 72 BMP, repeating the pattern four times instead of two. The long-term goal is to gradually increase your speed and endurance so you can play the entire drill, in all keys at four notes per beat, 132 BPM. As always, practice hands separately and then hands together. You are trying to achieve an effortless legato (smooth and connected) tone. Listen to the demo for guidance.

Blues Scales

The blues scale is one of the most used scales in contemporary music due to its melodic qualities. The formula for this scale is root, ♭3, 4, ♯4, 5, ♭7, root. In the key of C this would translate to C, E♭, F, F♯, G, B♭, C.

Example 37: C Blues Scale

TRACK 26

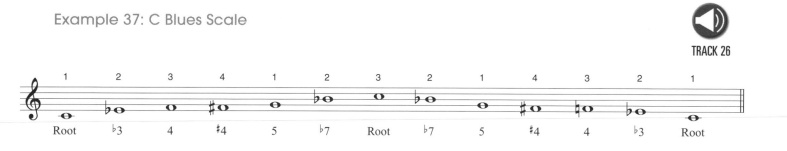

Blues Scale Drill

Learn the 12 blues scales two octaves in all keys. Play a dominant 7th chord in the left hand while playing the scale in the right.

Example 38: The 12 Blues Scales

C blues scale

G blues scale

D blues scale

A blues scale

E blues scale

B blues scale

F# blues scale

C# blues scale

F blues scale

B♭ blues scale

E♭ blues scale

A♭ blues scale

Harmony

Continue practicing your Key Regimen from the last lesson but now add Key Regimen step 4, *The Diatonic Major Progression*, to all keys. The chords for this progression are derived from the major scale of that key, hence the name **diatonic**, meaning "of or relating to the tones." In the key of C, this is simple as there are no sharps or flats and the notes in all of the chords are white keys. However, in other keys, be careful to play the appropriate accidentals. This will give you knowledge and facility with your basic chords in all keys. Practice this drill hands separately and hands together in all keys. If you need to, write this out first. Do not just do this drill robotically. Make sure you know what chord you are playing when you play it. You should practice this both in triads and tetrads.

Example 39: The Diatonic Major Progression

TRACK 28

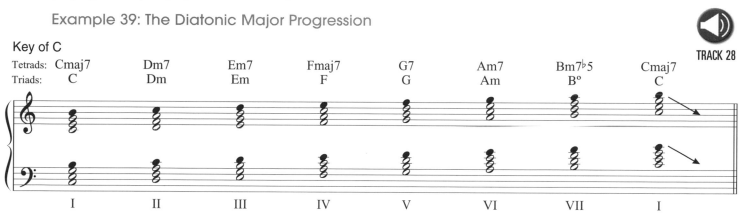

In the example above, notice that the top notes are black indicating this note was added to the basic triad to form tetrads.

Diatonic Pattern of Chords

Scale Degree Function	I	II	III	IV	V	VI	VII
Triads:	maj	min	min	maj	maj	min	dim
Tetrads:	maj7	m7	m7	maj7	dom7	m7	m7♭5

Rhythm

To master the nine basic rhythmic subdivisions, write out your own etude per the example below. Put the counts below the notes and practice the etude with a metronome until you can flawlessly play these rhythms in any combination. Write out as many etudes as is necessary to accomplish this goal. (Note: all rhythm studies should, at this point in your training, include your left hand playing quarter notes.)

Example 40: The Basic Rhythm Etude

TRACK 29

Improvisation

Okay, last lesson we just had a good time improvising with no rules. Now let's look at two types of improvising that once understood and mastered will serve you well in most any situation.

Key center: This type of improvising, in general, ignores the chord changes and concentrates on the key center (a mode or scale) with only occasional references to the chord changes—blues, rock, country, R&B, pop, etc. (See Example 41.)

Making the changes: This type of improvising, in general, concentrates on outlining the chord changes as they go by with only occasional references to the key center—jazz, fusion, classical, etc. (See Example 42.)

Example 41: Key Center Improvising

Example 42: Making the Changes

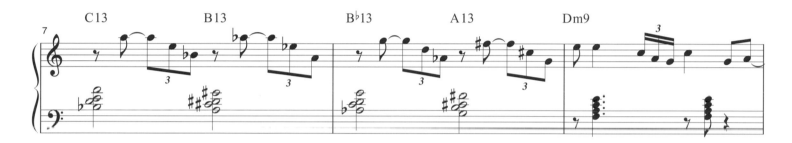

The Improvised Line: Any improvisation (melody) can for instructional purposes be broken down into four main categories:

1. *Chord tones*: The root, third, fifth, and seventh of the chord (R, 3, 5, 7). Please note since the 7 and 6 are interchangeable, then it could also be R, 3, 5, 7, or 6.

2. *Passing tones*: Scale tones that connect two adjacent chord tones (2, 4, and 6).

3. *Approach tones*: In general, and for now these are weak tones that approach the strong chord tones (1/2 step from below and scale degree from above are the most common).

4. *Tensions*: In general, a tension is any note that enriches (adds color or tension to) a basic chord sound (maj7, m7, dom7, etc.) without destroying its basic "color."

Example 43: The Improvised Line

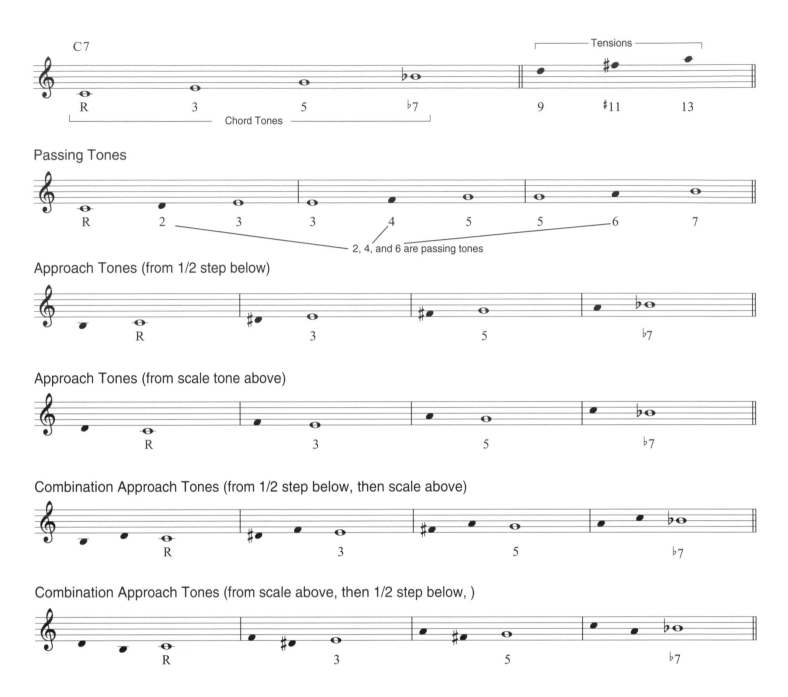

The goal is to not only know how to play these four categories of notes over any basic chord, but also to be able to hear them so they can be used in your improvisation. The following basic chord breakdowns should therefore be transposed and played in all keys. For even further progress, you should sing these exercises. First, sing along when you play them to teach your ear how they sound. Then, only play the root, and sing the exercises. Yes, this is a lot of work, but very valuable to your progress as an improviser.

Supplemental: See *The Contemporary Keyboardist*™, pp. 98–99, as well as the DVD *Part 2, Rhythm, Improvisation, and the Blues,* booklet pp. 16–17.

C Major 7

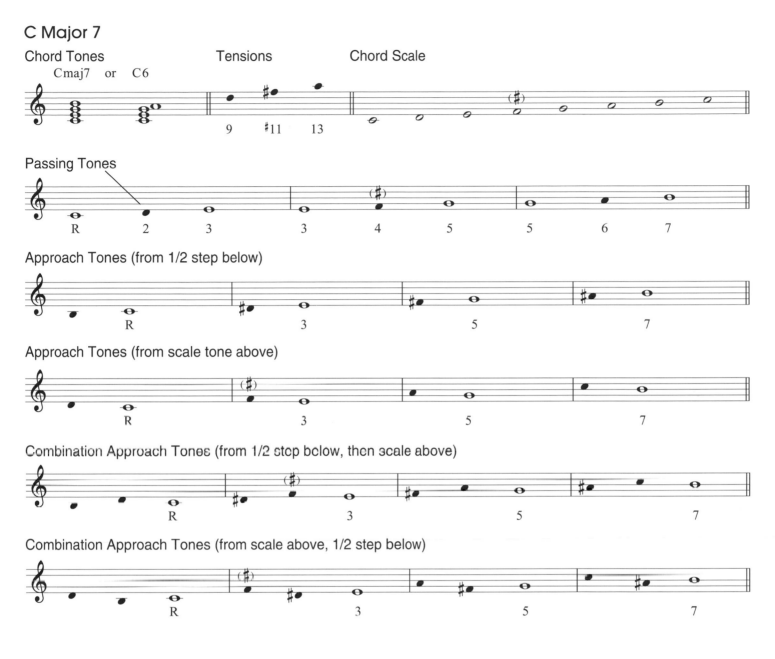

C Minor 7

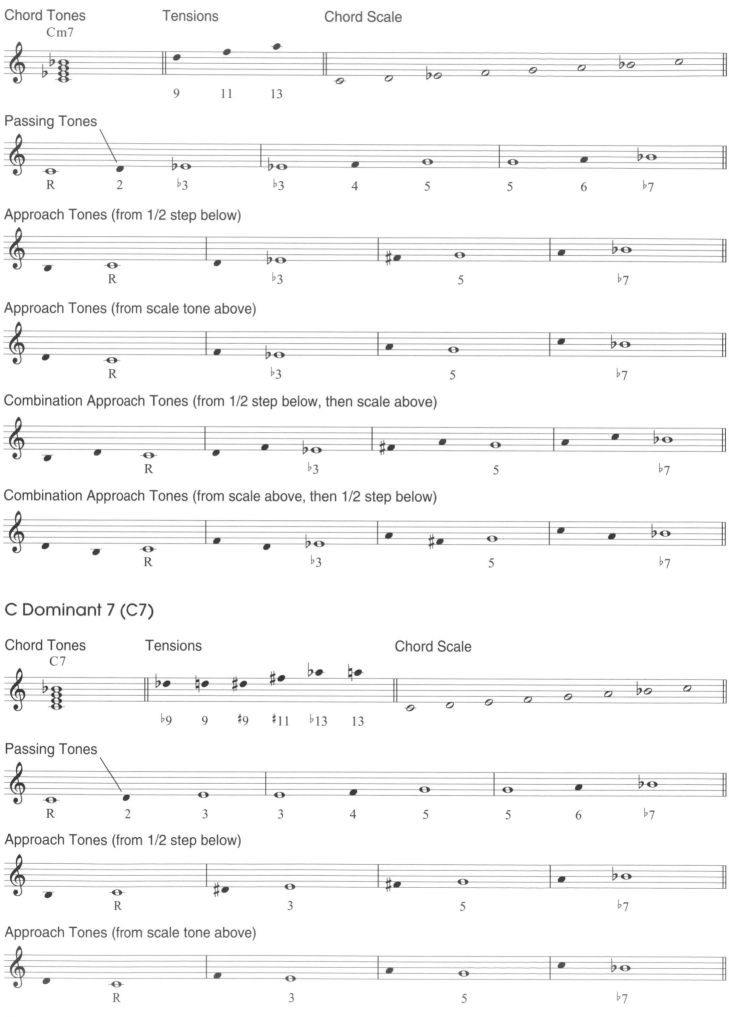

Chord Tones   Tensions   Chord Scale

Passing Tones

Approach Tones (from 1/2 step below)

Approach Tones (from scale tone above)

Combination Approach Tones (from 1/2 step below, then scale above)

Combination Approach Tones (from scale above, then 1/2 step below)

C Dominant 7 (C7)

Chord Tones   Tensions   Chord Scale

Passing Tones

Approach Tones (from 1/2 step below)

Approach Tones (from scale tone above)

Combination Approach Tones (from 1/2 step below, then scale above)

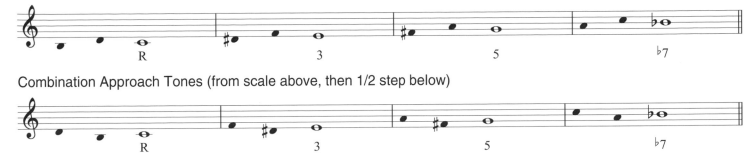

Combination Approach Tones (from scale above, then 1/2 step below)

C Minor 7♭5

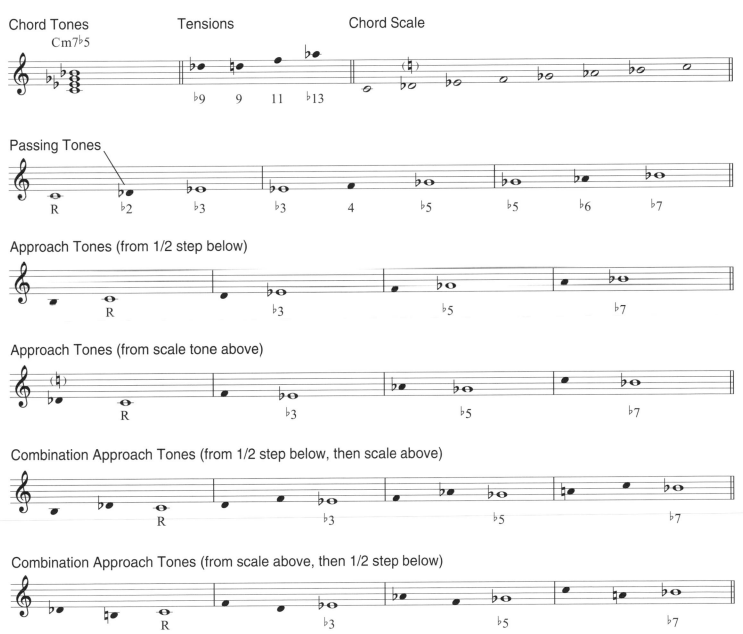

Chord Tones   Tensions   Chord Scale
Cm7♭5

♭9   9   11   ♭13

Passing Tones

R   ♭2   ♭3   ♭3   4   ♭5   ♭5   ♭6   ♭7

Approach Tones (from 1/2 step below)

R   ♭3   ♭5   ♭7

Approach Tones (from scale tone above)

R   ♭3   ♭5   ♭7

Combination Approach Tones (from 1/2 step below, then scale above)

R   ♭3   ♭5   ♭7

Combination Approach Tones (from scale above, then 1/2 step below)

R   ♭3   ♭5   ♭7

C Diminished 7

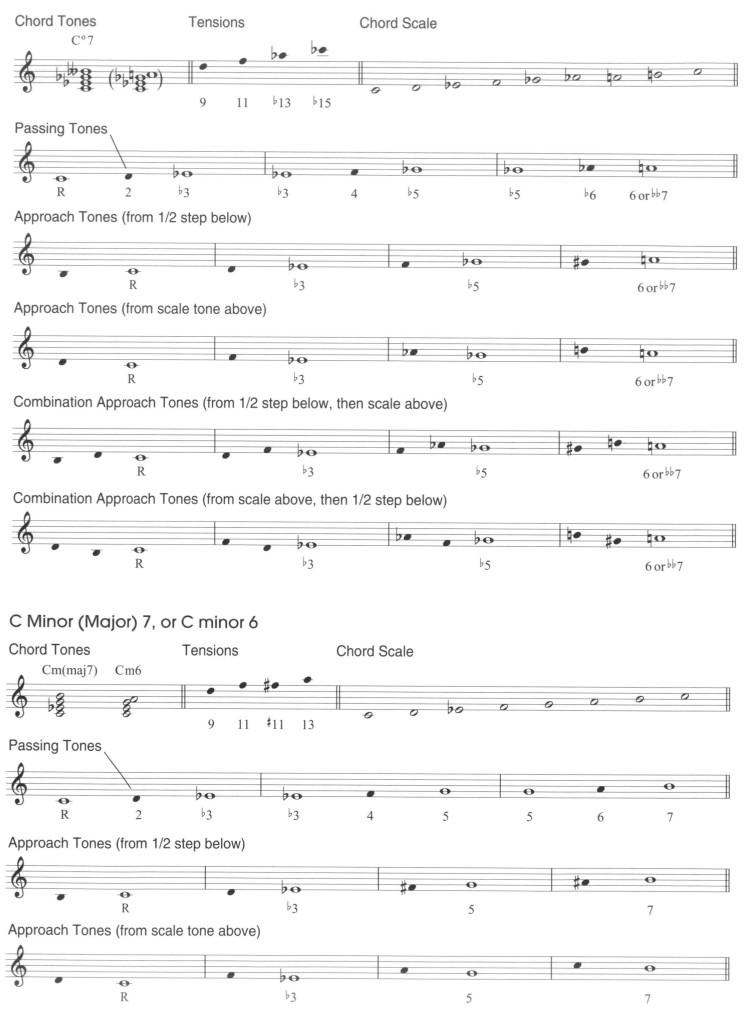

C Minor (Major) 7, or C minor 6

Combination Approach Tones (from 1/2 step below, then scale above)

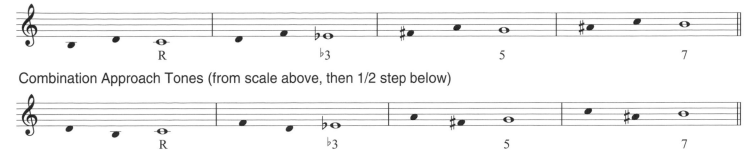

Combination Approach Tones (from scale above, then 1/2 step below)

Supplemental: See *The Contemporary Keyboardist*™, pp. 167–184, as well as DVD *Part 2, Rhythm, Improv, and the Blues*,
booklet pp. 18–23.

Repertoire

Listen to and learn the following etude (study). For even better results you should transpose this song
study to all keys.

Etude #2

TRACK 33

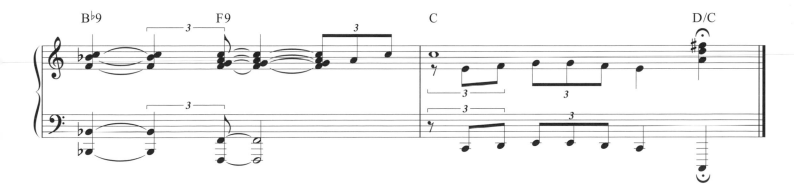

Practical

_____ 1. The II triad in the key of B♭ is _____; the VI tetrad in the key of D is _____; the V tetrad in the key of F♯ is _____; the IV triad in the key of B is _____; the VII tetrad in the key of D♭ is _____; the III tetrad in the key of E♭ is _____.

_____ 2. While your left hand plays quarter notes on the C below middle C, improvise using one note in the right hand, switching at will between the nine basic rhythms. This is exactly the same as the drill you did above Example 40, only you are improvising rhythmically, instead of playing an already written out etude.

_____ 3. What are the four categories of notes that can make up any melody or improvisation?

_____ 4. Analyze the following melody "Skippin'," as to both key center and making the changes. Define areas derived from blues scales and/or the improvised line categories. (Note: There is no sound byte for this example as this is an intellectual exercise.)

Skippin'

LESSON 9 • Blues Improvisation

Theory

Ear Training

Perfect Relative Pitch Drill, Full-Range

Continue the Perfect Relative Pitch drill as before but now practice it full-range. What this means is test yourself on the entire piano keyboard: high, low, middle, and at random. Eventually you will be able to determine the pitch no matter where it is on the keyboard because, after all, a D is a D is a D. It makes no difference whether it is a low or high D.

Technique

Speed Development: Continue the Five Finger Drill, working towards the goal of four notes per beat at 132 BPM, aiming for better endurance and clarity. This is a long-term drill and gets better with repetition.

Adding different rhythms: We are now ready to add rhythms 5 and 6 from the Nine Basic Rhythm Patterns, at a metronome setting of 112 BPM. Again, transpose these variations to all keys. After you learn them individually, change from rhythm #2 to rhythm #5, then to rhythm #6, at will.

Example 45a: Five Finger Drill, Rhythm #5

TRACK 34

Example 45b: Five Finger Drill, Rhythm #6

TRACK 35

The Chromatic Scale: This is a scale that includes all 12 notes or all colors. It should be learned in all keys once mastered in C, which is pretty easy as the fingering remains the same.

Example 46: The Chromatic Scale

TRACK 36

Harmony

Continue the Key Regimen but add step 5a—the diatonic progression in the circle of fifths. Harmonic motion in downwards fifths is a very common and musical chord progression in many songs and so learning this exercise will be very helpful. Notice the progression is now I–IV–VII–III–VI–II–V–I.

Example 47: Step 5a, The Diatonic Progression Circle of Fifths

TRACK 37

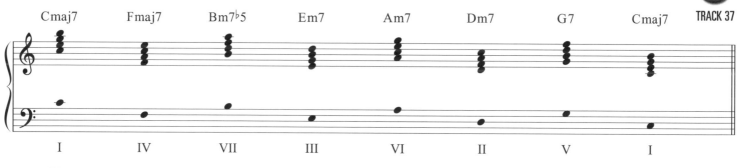

Rhythm

The Nine Basic Rhythms Tie Drill

By adding ties to the nine basic rhythms, many more complex rhythms can be created. If you have trouble initially playing these rhythms, play them first without the ties, and then try adding the ties.

Example 48: The Tie Drill

TRACK 38

Improvisation

Blues: To any musician, trained or untrained, the blues means a fairly fixed set of harmonic changes usually 12 bars in length. Over the years, these changes have been re-harmonized producing many variations. The first variation or form we will study is the basic I–IV–V blues, or "Form #1."

Example 49: The Basic (12 bar) Blues

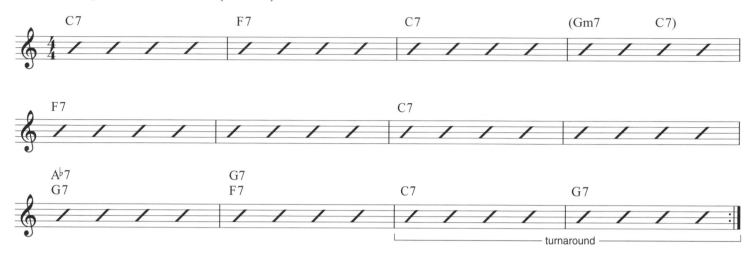

Note: The chords in parenthesis are optional variations for you to try later. The turnaround is the last two measures. It is called this because it is a progression that brings you back to the start of the blues. The last time through, however, you would play an ending, not a turnaround. The blues could be of any feel—swing, shuffle, rock, Latin, etc., and can be in any time signature such as 4/4, etc.

Example 50: Left-Hand Blues Pattern

This example shows one possible left-hand pattern played throughout the blues. There are many variations.

Supplemental: See DVD *Part 2, Rhythm, Improv, and the Blues*, booklet, pp. 24–29 for more on this blues form.

Repertoire

Listen to and learn the following etude. For even better results, transpose this song study to all keys.

Etude #3

TRACK 39

Practical

1. Sit in front of your keyboard and play an A major chord to get the A tonality in your mind's ear. Then, with your eyes closed, and with the eraser end of a pencil, hit any note anywhere on the piano and identify it. Continue doing this for ten minutes, noting how many notes you get right. Do this daily, with different key centers and compare your results each time.

2. Play the entire key regimen, steps 1 through 5a in all keys. Take your time as speed is not the goal here; familiarity with the key is.

3. As previously, reverse roles and play quarter notes in your right hand while your left hand plays example 48, the Tie Drill.

4. What is a turnaround? Where does the turnaround occur in a 12 bar blues?

5. While playing the left hand blues pattern in the key of C, try playing any notes from the C blues scale. Keep it simple, at first, until your independence between the hands develops. Once you can do it in C, you know what to do!

LESSON 10 • Intros, Turnarounds, and Endings

Theory

Ear Training

Since triads and tetrads make up basic harmony in contemporary popular music, we are now going to train the ear to recognize them.

Basic Triad Drill

TRACK 40

Given any note, be able to sing the following triads:

Major 1–3–5

Minor 1–♭3–5

Diminished 1–♭3–♭5

Augmented 1–3–♯5

Suspended 4th 1–4–5

Suspended 2nd 1–2–5

Procedure: Play any note on your keyboard, and then sing all the basic triads in random order. Make sure you check each note after you sing it to ensure you are singing the note correctly, and in tune.

Technique

Continue the Five Finger Drill as before, but now we are going to strengthen our technique even more by doing the Double Thirds Drill.

Example 51: The Double Thirds Drill

TRACK 41

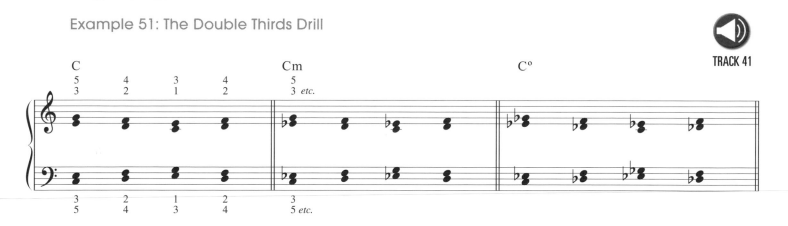

Procedure: The good news is that this drill is based on the same pattern from the five finger drill, the only difference being you are playing two notes (thirds) at a time in each hand. You should, as always, practice hands separately at first. Once you have learned the drill and can plays hands together, begin using the metronome eventually playing it at two notes per beat at 112 BPM.

Harmony

Key Regimen Step 5b: Continue practicing the Key Regimen but now add step 5b, the Diatonic Circle of Fifths Voice Led. *Voice led* means moving the chords to the next closest inversion for a smoother transition. This is very useful in actual playing and in accompanying a singer or other instrumentalist as it produces a more musical path through the chord progression. Notice that the progression is still I–IV–VII–III–VI–II–V–I, but now voice led. Practice in all keys.

Example 52: Step 5b, The Diatonic Circle of Fifths Voice Led

TRACK 42

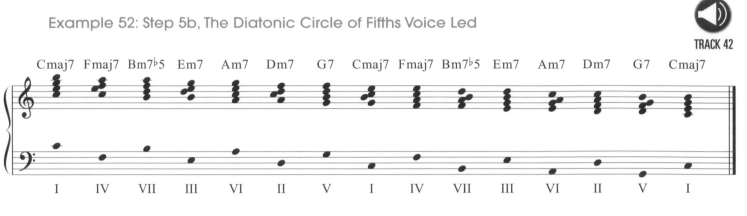

Rhythm

The Nine Basic Rhythms Rest Drill

By adding rests to the nine basic rhythms, many more complex rhythms can be created. Remember, rests are symbols denoting durations of silence, so in actuality you are getting rid of notes and replacing them with moments of silence. If you have trouble initially playing these rest rhythms, play them first without the rests, and then try adding the rests. Again, play left-hand quarter notes and remember to count correctly, even if only mentally.

Example 53: The Nine Basic Rhythms Rest Drill

TRACK 43

Improvisation

The *blues* sound is basically composed of two elements: 1) The *blues scale*, which we learned in an earlier lesson and; 2) *blue tones*, which are crushed non-diatonic notes that approach scale tones, but most often chord tones. The *blue tone licks* in Example 54 are all based off of C7 but should be transposed to the other two chords F7 and G7 in form one, and practiced over the left-hand pattern. These should get you started, but, in the end, you'll need to create your own licks. (See CD Track #44.)

Example 54: Stylistic Blues Licks

Intros, Turnarounds, and Endings: These can really spice up the blues. They should be practiced and memorized so they can be used at will. Please note that an intro or turnaround always ends on the V7 chord; in this case, G7 in the key of C, to set up the I chord (C7) in measure one. An ending usually ends on the tonic or I chord (C7). Most are two measures long, but sometimes they are four measures in length. There are endless possibilities, but these few will get you going.

Example 55: Blues Intros and Turnarounds

Example 56: Blues Endings

TRACK 46

Supplemental: For a more comprehensive look at the blues, see *The Contemporary Keyboardist*™, pp. 345–362 as well as the DVD *Part 2, Rhythm, Improv, and the Blues*, booklet pp. 24-39.

Repertoire

Listen to and learn the following etude. For even better results, transpose this song study to all keys.

Etude #4

TRACK 47

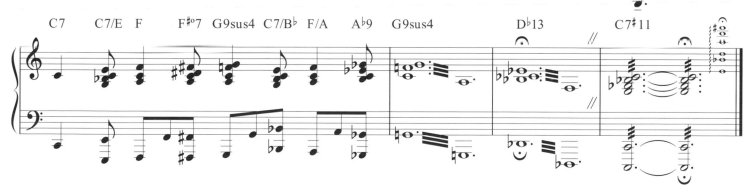

Practical

_____ 1. Write out, in all keys, the tetrad names for the **I–IV–VII–III–VI–II–V–I** progression. (For example, Key of C: Cmaj7, Fmaj7, Bm7♭5, Em7, etc.)

_____ 2. Reverse roles and play quarter notes in your right hand while your left hand plays Example 48, "The Tie Drill."

_____ 3. What two elements is the blues sound composed of?

_____ 4. Learn all the stylistic blues licks in Example 54 in the key of C and incorporate them in your blues improvisations. Make sure you incorporate the intros, turnarounds, and endings in Examples 55 and 56. Once the blues in the key of C is mastered, begin jamming in other keys. The blues is a good format to use when jamming with other musicians, and so you should always be ready to blow!

LESSON 11 • Advanced Voicings

Theory

Ear Training

TRACK 48

The Scat and Play Drill

The purpose of this drill is to get your internal ear hooked up to your playing by Scatting (singing) any note in your vocal range and then trying to find (play) it on your keyboard. If you get it wrong on the first attempt, re-try until you get it right. Eventually, you will magically just know where the note is, as the drill hones in your psychic ear.

Procedure: Scat (sing) any note within your vocal range. Then put your hand over the keyboard and let your inner ear direct you to the correct note. Play the note even if you're not sure. Let your intuition guide you, wrong or right. If it is wrong, try again and again until you seem to effortlessly "know" what note it is.

Technique

The Double Thirds Drill

In order to strengthen endurance and velocity of single-note playing, begin practicing the double thirds drill at MM = 62, four notes per beat, four times through the pattern. First, warm up doing two notes per beat at 112, two times through the pattern as before. Then, play four times through the pattern at 62. Each week, try and increase the tempo until you reach MM = 100, four notes/beat, four times through the pattern. This may take a while, but the resultant headroom in your technique is worth the effort. Finally, try it at four notes per beat, four times through each pattern at 72–100 BPM.

TRACK 49

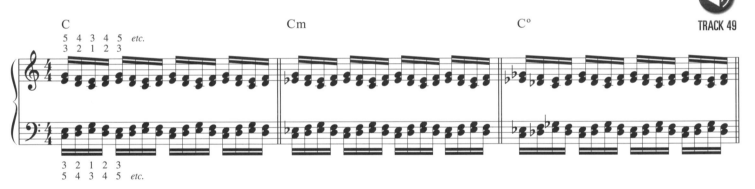

Example 57: The Double Thirds Drill (Four notes per beat)

Procedure: Play at 62–112, two notes per beat, two times through each pattern. Next, play at 62–100, four notes per beat, four times through each pattern.

Harmony

Theory of Advanced Chord Structures: Advanced chord structures are basic chord structures (triads and tetrads) with added tensions. A *tension*, in general, is any tone that enriches a basic chord without destroying its basic quality (major 7, minor 7, etc.). The most used of these tones are intervals of 9s, 11s, and 13s. The following chart shows the available tensions that go with each chord quality. What tensions a composer or a player adds to basic chords is a matter of two things: the melody and individual choice per the color or tension desired. (Note: In general, simpler music such as pop, country, and rock use tensions sparingly, whereas, jazz, funk, blues, and fusion use tensions frequently.) There's no need at this time to memorize these tensions. Just refer to this chart as necessary. The more important thing is to hear how these tensions are used so you can use them!

Example 58: Tension Chart

Chord Quality	Available Tensions
C, C6, Cmaj7	9, #11, 13
Cm, Cm7	9, 11, 13
C7	♭9, 9, #9, #11, ♭13, 13
Cm7♭5	♭9, 9, 11, ♭13
C°7	9, 11, ♭13, ♭15
Cm6, Cm(maj7)	9, 11, #11, 13

Supplemental: See "Tensions," in *The Contemporary Keyboardist*™, pp. 96–97.

Advanced Chord Construction: Now that you understand tensions, it's time to learn the procedure to add these to your basic chords in order to create and play advanced chords.

Rules: The following apply in creating four-note chord voicings with tensions:

1. All Tension 9s substitute for the root.

2. All tension 11s and 13s substitute for the 5th.

Exception: On chords with a flatted 5th (m7♭5 and diminished 7th), all tensions substitute only for the root as the flatted 5th is a defining chord tone.

Creating Advanced Chords: To create these, simply substitute each tension asked for, one at a time, using the above rules.

Procedure: C7♭9(♭13) is really a C 7th chord with two additional tensions added to it for color. Therefore, the flat 9 of C is D flat. Rule 1 applies, so substitute D flat for the root. Next, the flat 13th in C is A flat so Rule 2 applies so substitute A flat for G, the fifth. The advanced chord is now (E, A♭, B♭, D♭) which translates to (3, ♭13, ♭7, ♭9). Study the advanced chords in Example 59 so you fully understand the procedure. Since any four-note chord has four different positions, it does not matter what order your notes are. This is called "voicing" a chord, and it's purely a matter of taste and musicality—what sounds good!

Example 59: Advanced Chords

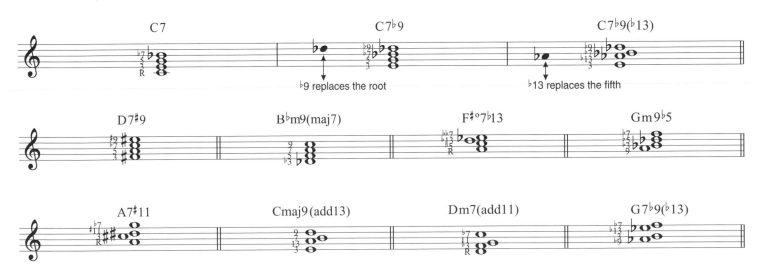

Supplemental: For a more expanded look into advanced chords and other voicings, read chapters 8, 12 and 13 in *The Contemporary Keyboardist*™, and see the DVD *Part 1, The Basics*, page 34.

Rhythm Combination Tie and Rest Etude: By adding ties and rests to the nine basic rhythms, many complex rhythms can be created. Study and learn Example 60 by playing left-hand quarter notes and right-hand rhythms. Make sure you count. If you are having any trouble, first play the rhythm without the tie or rest.

Example 60: The Rhythm Combination Tie and Rest Etude

TRACK 50

Improvisation

Blues Form #2 (Jazz): This form of the blues uses the II–V progression in measure four to set up the IV chord in measure five. It also uses the II–V progression in measures 9 and 10 to set up the turnaround in measures 11 and 12. Although it more readily lends itself to jazz improvisation than Form #1, it is still a blues, and so the blues scale sound should still be the dominant approach in my opinion. Notice in both blues forms that the IV chord in measure 5 is always intact.

Example 61: Blues Form #2

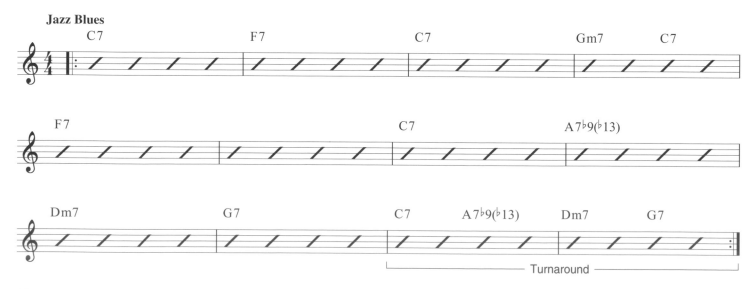

Repertoire: Listen to and learn the following etude. For even better results, transpose this song study to all keys.

Etude #5

TRACK 51

Supplemental: *The Contemporary Keyboardist*™, page 29.

Practical

_____ 1. Why do you think it is important to let your inner ear direct your playing?

_____ 2. What's the main difference between a basic chord quality and an advanced chord quality?

_____ 3. Define tension.

_____ 4. What are the two rules that govern the addition of tensions to a four part basic chord? Why, on chords with a flat five (example Cm7♭5 or C°7), is there an exception to these two rules?

_____ 5. Construct the following advanced chords: Bdim7(9), A♭m7(9), D7♯9, Am(maj7♯11), E♭maj7(9) (13), G7♭13(9), Cm7♭5(11), F♯m7(9)(13), D♭7♯11, B♭maj7(♯11)

_____ 6. Again, as previously, reverse roles and play quarter notes in your right hand while your left hand plays Example 60, the Tie and Rest Etude.

_____ 7. Transpose the changes of Blues Form #2 to all keys. Each week, spend a little time in a different key practicing your blues licks, blues scale and jazz improvisation over a different blues key. There's no excuse for not being able to eventually play this blues in all keys.

Theory

Ear Training

TRACK 52

The Scat and Play Drill Phrases

Same purpose and procedure as the "One Note Scat and Play" drill from the last lesson, only this time, sing three- or four-note phrases, and then try to play them. You should not proceed with this drill until the "One Note Scat and Play" drill is mastered.

Technique

The Five Finger Trill Drill

Purpose: To strengthen the 5th and 4th fingers.

Procedure: Play the Trill Drill as written, using the same pattern from the regular five finger drill. Start slowly and gradually increase the tempo to 132 BPM four notes per beat, four times through the pattern.

Example 62: The Five Finger Trill Drill

TRACK 53

Harmony

The II–V Progression: Understanding this progression is essential for understanding contemporary popular harmony. The essence of music and the journey it takes us on is tension and release. The rhythms thus created by tension and release are called *harmonic rhythms*. A harmonic rhythm is the rhythm resulting from the movement of chords, one to the next. The whole reason why chords tend to move or stay at rest is based on tension and release. The less stable a chord is, the more it wants to resolve its notes or voices (known as "voice leading") to another chord. Chords that tend to stay at rest may be described as static in nature, while chords that are unstable and thus want to move on can be described as tense in nature. Understanding this principle allows the performing musician, as well as the songwriter, to use the best possible harmonies for the desired effect.

Example 63: C Major Diatonic Progression

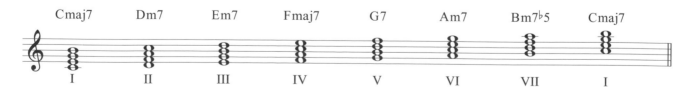

Although each chord in the example above is a stand-alone entity unto itself, it can further be grouped into categories that have specific behavioral patterns relative to the principles of tension and release.

Example 64: Tension/Release Categories

Categories	Chords	Tension/Release Index
Tonic (static)	I, III, VI	Stable, no real tendency to move on; release
Subdominant (axis)	II, IV	Not very stable, tendency to resolve or axis (pivot) to another chord; tense
Dominant (tense)	V, VII	Very unstable, strong tendency to resolve; very tense

Note: Although not the subject of this book, in later advanced lessons we will look at how this categorical thinking facilitates reharmonization—the substitution of new chords for basic ones.

Notice how the II–V–I progression fulfills the tension and release requirements of all three categories.

II = subdominant = axis (moving)

V = dominant = very tense

I = tonic = static (very stable)

Progressions of this nature are known as **cadences**. A cadence is a harmonic progression which suggests a conclusion, if only temporary. The II–V–I progression is a **full** or **perfect cadence** because of its finality (Example 65a). Other cadences derived from these categories or colors are known as **Imperfect** or **half cadences**: tonic to dominant or V–I (Example 65b); the church or **plagal cadence**: subdominant to tonic or IV–I (Example 65c); the **deceptive** or **interrupted cadence**: dominant to some other chord other than the tonic (Example 65d). These cadences, along with their many variations, constitute to a large extent the basis of traditional and contemporary tonal harmony.

Examples 65a – 65d: Cadences

TRACK 54

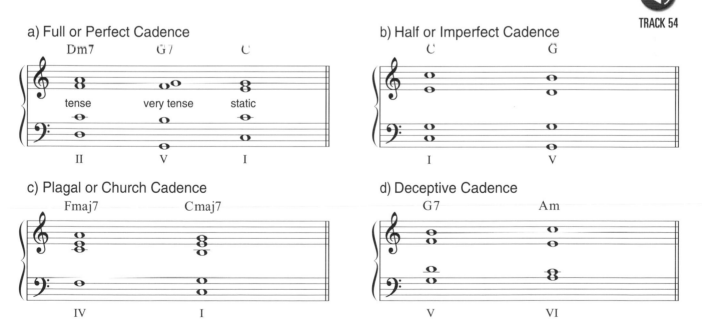

a) Full or Perfect Cadence

Dm7   G7   C

tense   very tense   static

II   V   I

b) Half or Imperfect Cadence

C   G

I   V

c) Plagal or Church Cadence

Fmaj7   Cmaj7

IV   I

d) Deceptive Cadence

G7   Am

V   VI

Supplemental: See *The Contemporary Keyboardis*™, pp. 205–220 for a more comprehensive look at advanced harmony.

With this background, you are now ready to learn your II–V–I advanced progressions. I say "advanced," because these chords have tensions added to them as was discussed in Lesson 11. In the key of C, for example, the II chord was Dm7, but now it's Dm7(9) or Dm9. The V chord was G7, but now it's G7(9)(13), or G13. The I chord was C major 7, but it was changed to C6(9), (see Example 66).

Remember, advanced chords are those basic chords that have been made more colorful by adding tensions to them.

Example 66: II–V–I Advanced Chord Voicings

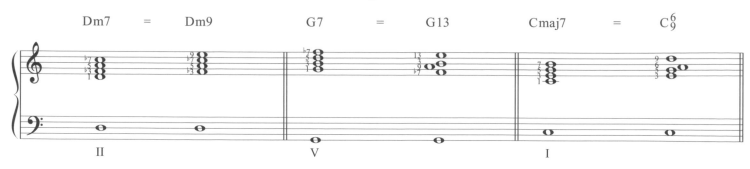

II–V–I Major Key Drill: Learn the following II–V–I progressions by:

    a) Playing the drill exactly as is:

          1. Left hand plays the root of the chord; right hand plays the chord voicing.

          2. Left hand plays the chord voicing by itself.

    b) Be able to, on command, play the II–V–I of any key.

    c) Be able to play any chord voicing from any key out of context of the II–V–I progression—for example, Gm9, B♭6(9), G7♭9(♭13), Am9, etc.

Note: The keys F♯ through B use a different inversion because, if the original inversion was continued, it would be too thin sounding and get in the way of the right hand.

Example 67: The II–V–I Major Progressions

TRACK 55

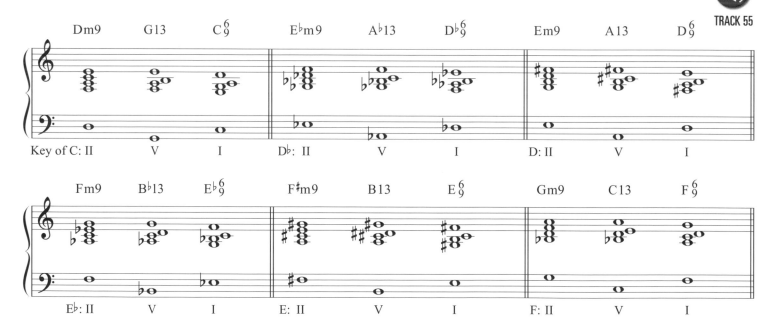

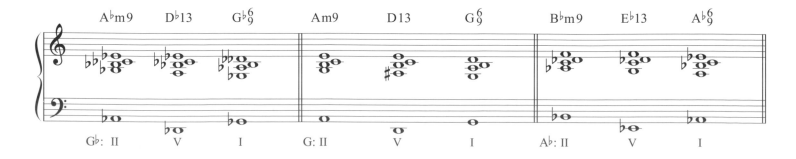

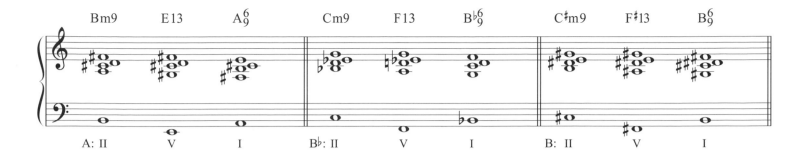

II–V–I Minor Key Drill: Now I hate to tell you this, but you now need to do the same exact drill and procedure, only with the II-V-I Minor keys!!!

Learn the following II–V–I minor progressions and use the same procedure as in the major II–V–I drill, steps a, b, and c.

Example 68: The II–V–I Minor Progressions

TRACK 56

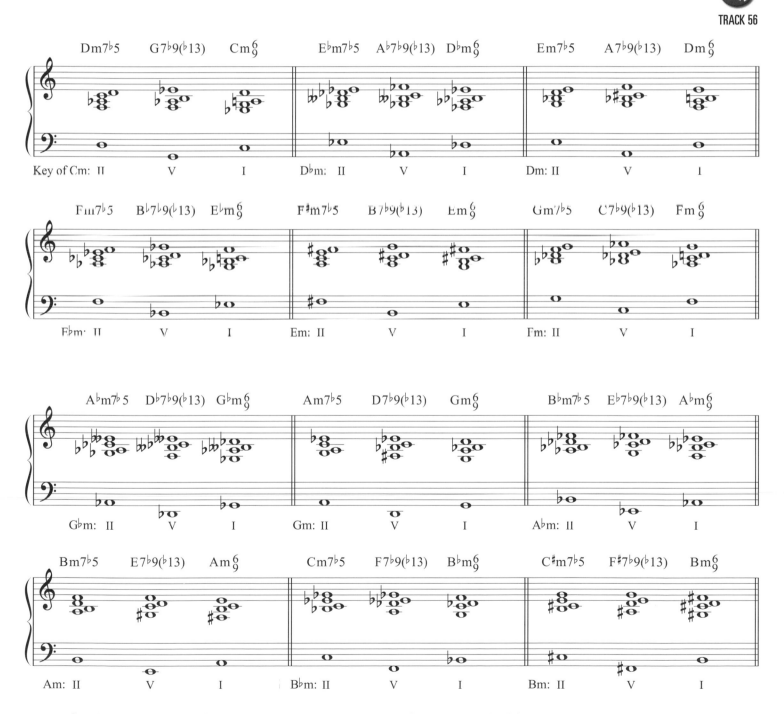

Supplemental: See *The Contemporary Keyboardist*™, pp. 91–95 for more on II–V voicings.

Rhythm

Polyrhythms: Rhythmic independence is the ability to hear and perform two or more rhythms at the same time. Two or more rhythms played simultaneously are called polyrhythms. They may be thought of as two different meters (time signatures) played against each other. Theoretically, you have already learned some basic polyrhythms when you did the "Nine Basic Rhythms" drill—two against one, three against one, and four against one.

Example 69: Basic Polyrhythms

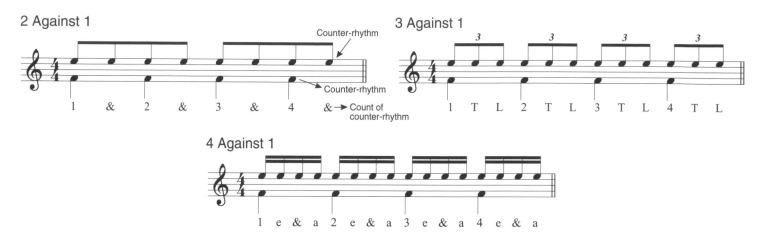

Although these are indeed polyryhthms, they are not very difficult, as they are all over a basic pulse subdivision of "one," which you have already practiced. However, the next three that we will cover—3 against 2, 3 against 4, and 4 against 3—are a bit more difficult due to the fact that the basic pulse subdivision is not 1, but 2, 4, and 3. In order to master these, the following procedure should be used:

1. Use a metronome, drum machine, or some fixed pulse to keep the basic beat absolutely consistent while you concentrate on playing, and ultimately hearing the counter-rhythm.

2. Count the exercise as indicated in order to fully understand it. (Note: The first part of each polyrhythm shows how it is actually counted and played; the second part shows how it is written.)

3. Continue steps 1 and 2 until the relationship of the rhythmic patterns is fully heard and felt. You will only then be able to use your own time (groove) without the aid of a fixed time aid.

4. Once duplicated, you should memorize the sound of the particular polyrhythm for quick future use.

By adding ties and rests to polyrhythms as we did with the nine basic rhythms, many more complex rhythms can be created. These are more advanced than the scope of this book.

Example 70: 3 Against 2

TRACK 57

Example 71: 3 Against 4

TRACK 58

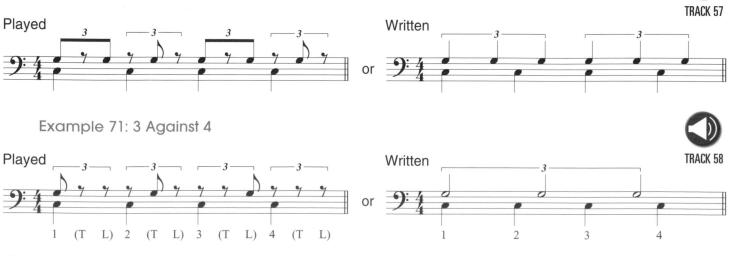

Example 72: 4 Against 3

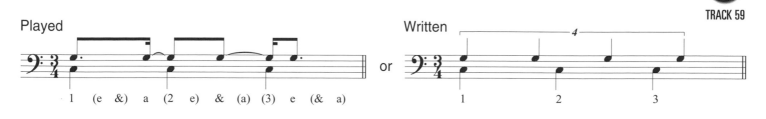

Played

1 (e &) a (2 e) & (a) (3) e (& a)

Written

or

1   2   3

Supplemental: See *The Contemporary Keyboardist*™, pp. 153–159.

Improvisation

Soloing over one chord (modal playing): Soloing over one chord creates a different challenge than soloing over chord changes. Initially, it seems like this would be simpler. But, in all honesty, it can actually be more difficult, as the challenge is to make your lines interesting even though you only have one chord and scale from which to draw. Of course, in the end, there's no substitute for just hearing good lines. But, to help get you to that point, remember these tools: chord scale permutations, the improvised line categories (chord tones, passing tones, approach tones, and tensions), and motivic playing.

1. **Chord Scale Permutations:** This simply means being able to improvise freely using the scale that goes with the chord in question. (See Chord Breakdowns in Lesson #8). For purposes of demonstration, C7 and its chord scale are used in the following examples. These permutations can and should be done on any chord scale you are trying to master. They should be done over the range of at least two octaves, up and down. Notice that permutation #5 is really "free soloing," using any interval from the scale you so desire. Of course, there are many more possibilities, but these will get you started.

Example 73: C7 Chord Scale and Permutations

Permutation #1: Melodic thirds

Permutation #2: Melodic fourths

Permutation #3: Melodic double thirds

Permutation #4: Melodic double fourths

Permutation #5: Melodic free form

Note: On the CD, an "advanced" form of the C7 chord is sounded—a C13 chord.

Chord Scale and Permutations

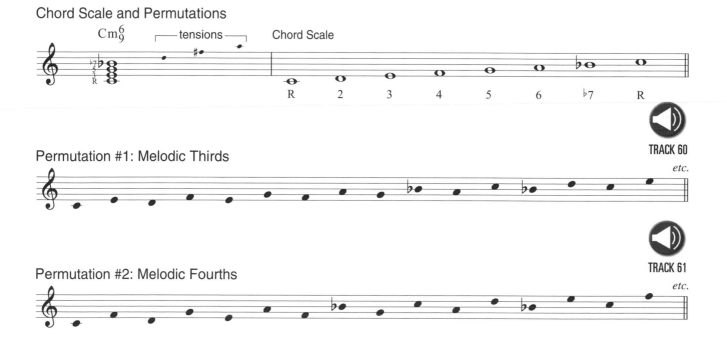

Permutation #3: Melodic Double Thirds

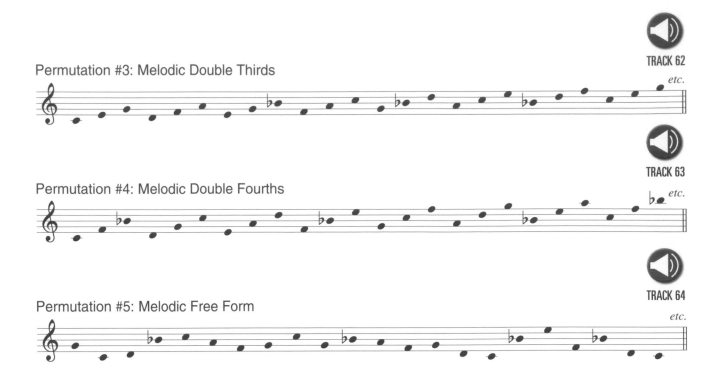

etc.

Permutation #4: Melodic Double Fourths

etc.

Permutation #5: Melodic Free Form

etc.

2. **Improvised Line Categories**: This is basically jazz improvisation. So, besides permutating notes from the actual chord scale (Note: a chord scale is simply chord tones plus passing tones), you can also add approach tones and tensions to your soloing. This will give you some nondiatonic notes (notes not in the chord scale) which will add a little color (spice) to your soloing!

Example 74: Jazz Improvisation Soloing Over One Chord

3. **Motific Playing**: This is my favorite tool as it adds musicality! This is simply playing a short phrase and stating it again a few times in different variations. Since the listener hears the motif and recognizes it when it is played again, it helps bring form and familiarization to your solo.

Example 75: Motific Playing

Etude #6

Practical

_____ 1. Listen to a song of your choice from any recording. Stop the recording, sing the phrase back to be sure you have it duplicated and then find it on the piano. Doing this often will help not only your ear but your repertoire of licks. (Note: If you sing it back incorrectly, then listen to the phrase again until you get it correct before you attempt to find it on the piano). This is an extension of the "Scat and Play Phrase" drill.

_____ 2. Define _harmonic rhythm_.

_____ 3. What is the difference between a *static* chord and a *tense* chord? Explain in your own words the relationship of tension and release in music.

_____ 4. What are the three basic harmonic categories relative to tension and release? Define their specific behavioral patterns.

_____ 5. What is a *cadence*? What are the three basic types of cadences?

_____ 6. Why is the II–V–I such a complete cadence?

_____ 7. There are 12 major keys and three chords in each key make up a II–V–I progression. That makes 36 advanced chord voicings. Cut up 36 one inch squares of paper and on one side put the name of the chord; for example, B6(9), C13, or Dm9, etc. Put these 36 squares in a bowl and pick them out at random one at a time. Try and play the chord as quickly as you can. Chords that take you longer than a few seconds put in pile A (the "to be studied more" pile), but only after you look then up and play them correctly. Chords that you get right away go into pile B, because you know them. Doing this every day is a quick way of learning your chord voicings.

_____ 8. Do the same drill as in #7 above, but with your II–V–I minor voicings.

_____ 9. Write a one chord improvisation over Dm7 using chord scale permutations, jazz improvisation categories, and motific concepts.

LESSON 13 • Jazz Improvisation

Theory

Ear Training

Melodic Transposition Drill

Purpose: To further train and coordinate the ear-mind-body-playing mechanism to play what it hears.

Procedure: Pick a melody that you already know and can sing out loud. (The quality of your voice is unimportant but your ability to sing the melody correctly is.) Using two hands and an octave apart, play the melody by ear, each time starting on a different beginning pitch. No thinking or intellectualizing is allowed. This is done totally by intuitive ear. Trying to memorize the intervals of the melody, such as up a half step or down a third, etc., defeats the purpose of allowing the ear to run the show. Play slowly and in time, trying all kinds of melodies: nursery rhymes, Christmas carols, standards, or whatever you can sing well. These are the types of melodies you should start off with. Eventually, you can graduate to more difficult melodies as your ear improves. But, make sure you know the melody and can sing it before you make an attempt. If you run out of melodies, then learn some new ones and then do the drill.

Technique

Each basic chord has a scale that goes with it. These are called chord scales. A chord scale is made up of the chord's chord tones (1,3,5,7) and its passing tones (2,4,6). Chord tones plus passing tones = the chord scale.

Example 76: Chord Scale Construction

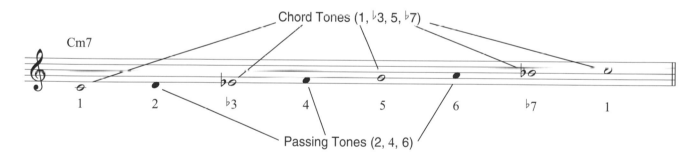

Example 77: Common Chord Scales

The following chord scales should be practiced two octaves all keys with the indicated left hand voicings. Knowing these chord scales will help your improvisational abilities so when you see these chord symbols, you will already know the available scale which is 50% of the available notes for improvisation, the other 50% being approach tones and tension tones. Practice all scales in the key of C first as indicated, and then, one key at a time, transpose them. It takes as long as it takes, so be thorough.

C6(9): C Major Scale

C13: C Mixolydian Scale

C7♯9(♭13): C Altered Dominant Scale

C7♯9(13): C Symmetrical Diminished Half-Whole Scale

C7♭9: C Dominant ♭9 Scale

C7♯5(9): C Whole Tone Scale

Cm9: C Dorian Scale

Cm7♭5: C Locrian Scale

C°7: C Symmetrical Diminished Whole-Half Scale

Cm6(9): C Melodic Minor Ascending Scale

C Major Scale

TRACK 69

C Mixolydian Scale

TRACK 70

C Altered Dominant Scale

TRACK 71

C Symmetrical Diminished Half-Whole Scale

TRACK 72

C Dominant ♭9 Scale

TRACK 73

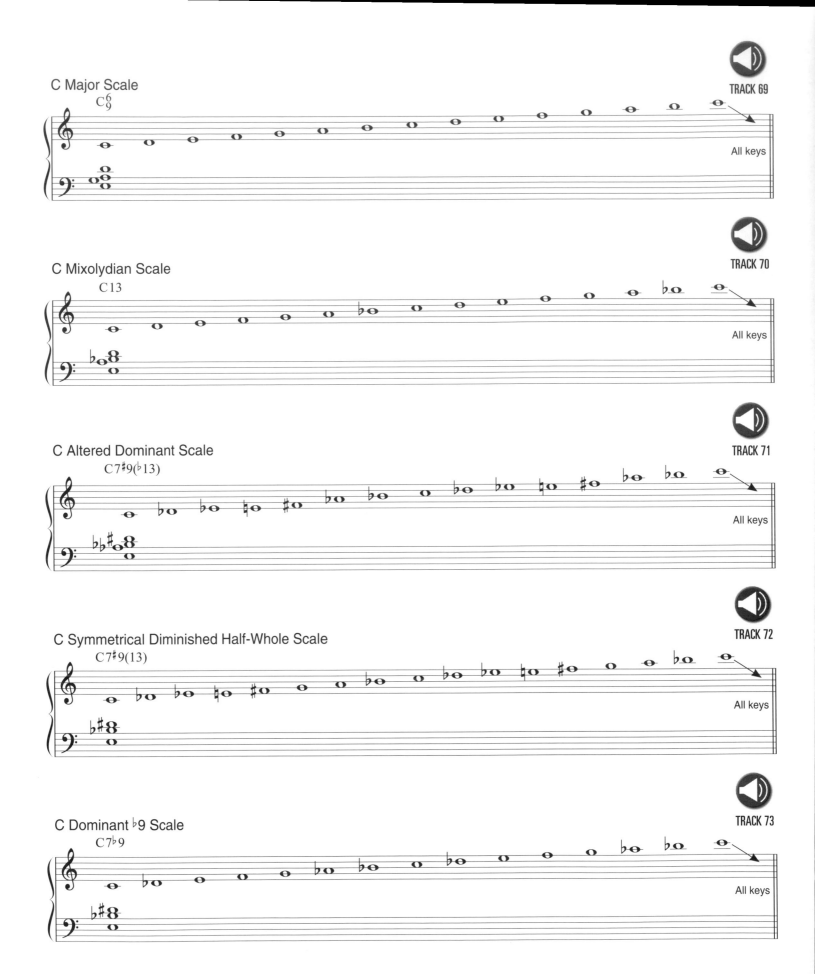

C Whole Tone Scale

TRACK 74

C7#5(9)

All keys

C Dorian Scale

TRACK 75

Cm9

All keys

C Locrian Scale

TRACK 76

Cm7♭5

All keys

C Symmetrical Diminished Whole-Half Scale

TRACK 77

C°7(9)

All keys

C Melodic Minor Scale (Ascending)

TRACK 78

Cm6/9

All keys

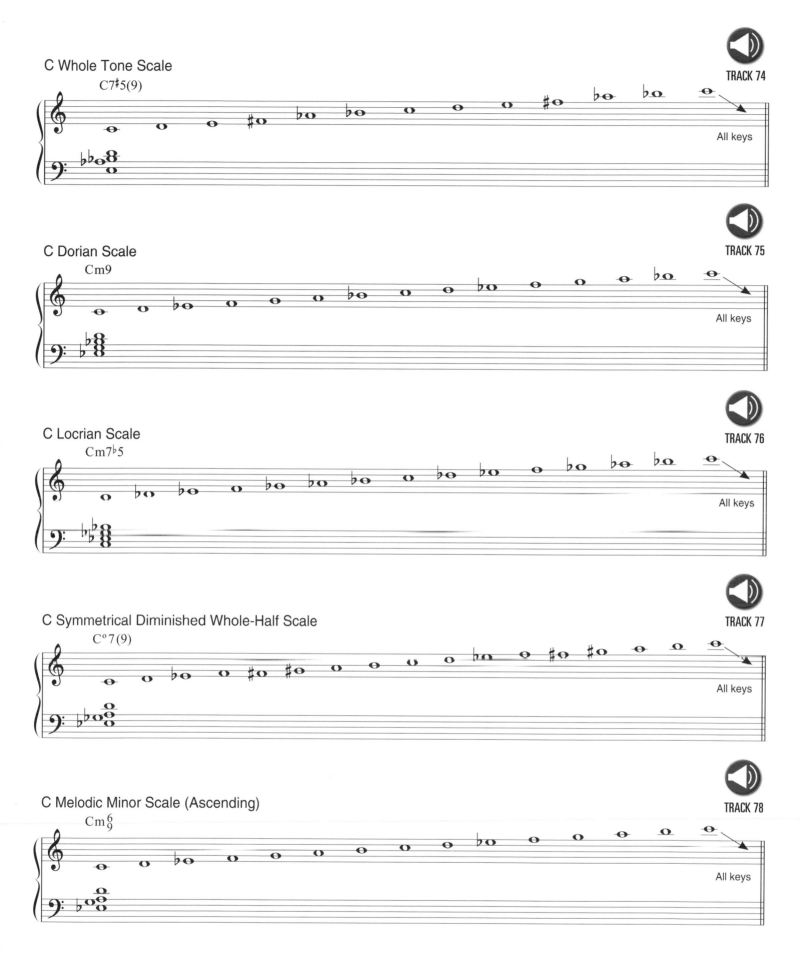

Supplemental: See *The Contemporary Keyboardist*™, pp. 185–189.

Harmony

In this lesson, we will look at how to convert basic chords, especially from fake books, to advanced chords. More often than not, charts/lead sheets indicate the basic chords of a song and leave it up to the player to fill in the spice. For example, a VI–II–V–I progression such as: **Dm7** / **Gm7 C7** / **Fmaj7** could be played **Dm9** / **Gm9 C7♭9(♭13)** / **F6(9)**.

The performer, with his/her ear, taking into consideration the style of music and the musical context, is actually expected to enhance these basic chords and licks as is necessary. Commercial music is, in the end, about feel, and nobody wants to write everything out all the time. The following basic chord conversion chart can be used to enhance any basic chord, but be careful to use these conversions tastefully. In other words, if the style of music was straight country rock, I doubt enhancing a G major chord to a Gmaj9♯11 would work, and conversely if the style was jazz bebop and you played a basic G7 as written instead of a G13 or a G7♯9♭13, well... you get the idea. This taste only comes with experience and lots of listening to many musical styles.

Basic Chord Conversion Chart: The following chart shows the basic chord qualities and their possible advanced chord options. The Theory of Advanced Chord Construction in Lesson 11 should be reviewed if there are any questions how basic chords are converted to advanced chords. The purpose of this chart is to clarify some of the possibilities. The chord progression that follows will give you an example of how these are converted.

Example 78: Basic Chord Conversion Chart

TRACK 79

Basic Chords	Advanced Chords
C, C6, Cmaj7	C6/9
Cm7	Cm9
C7, C9	C13
C7♭9	C7♭9(♭13) or C7♯9(♭13)
C7♯5	C9♯5
Cm7♭5	Cm7♭5
C°7	C°7
C7sus4	Gm9/C
Cm, Cm6, Cm(maj7)	Cm6/9

In the following, the root is left out in the "advanced chords." The root would normally be played with the left hand.

This example is the chord progression and melody to the jazz standard "Dear Old Stockholm," showing the conversion from basic chords to advanced.

Dear Old Stockholm

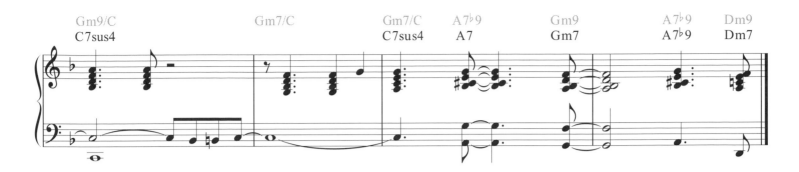

Rhythm

Advanced Rhythms: Now that we have studied dividing a beat into 2s, 3s, and 4s, it's time to look at the more advanced subdivisions of 5s, 6s, 7s, and 8s. Although used less frequently, they still come up from time to time, and should be mastered. The following are Basic Rhythms 10, 11, 12, and 13.

Example 80: Advanced Rhythm Subdivisions

Rhythm #10 Subdivision in 5 (Sixteenth note gets 1/5 of a count)

Rhythm #11 Subdivision in 6 (Sixteenth note gets 1/6 of a count)

Rhythm #12 Subdivision in 7 (Sixteenth note gets 1/7 of a count)

Rhythm #13 Subdivision in 8 (These are referred to as 32nd notes. Therefore, eight 32nd notes = one beat)

TRACK 81

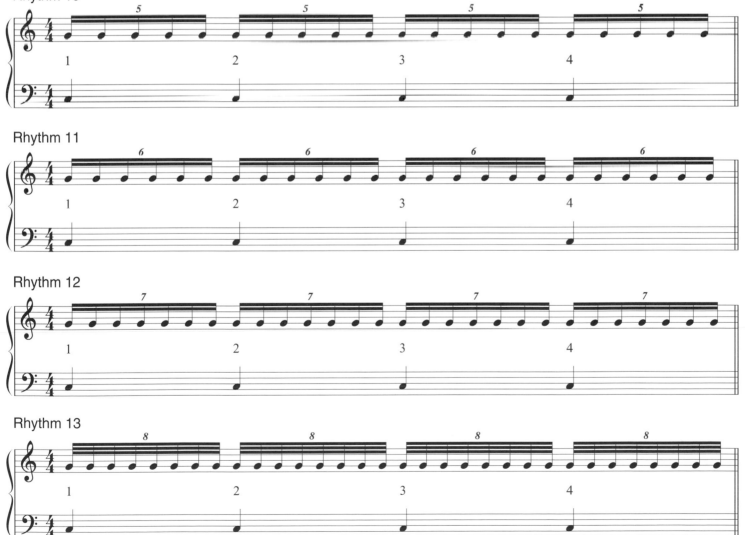

Improvisation

Jazz Improvisation: In Lesson 8, we discussed two types of improvisation, "key center" (blues/modal) and "making the changes" (jazz). Although one can play blues over a jazz tune, playing jazz would be more appropriate. To do this, one would use notes mostly from the four categories—chord tones, passing tones, approach tones and tensions. The following jazz improvisation contains II–V–I progressions, both major and minor. Note the left-hand jazz advanced voicings as we discussed earlier.

Example 81: Jazz Improvisation

Jazz Improvisation

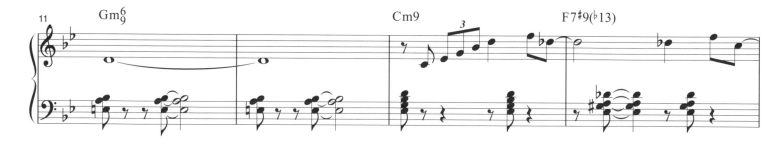

Supplemental: See *The Contemporary Keyboardist*™, pp. 107–114.

Repertoire

Etude #7: For your final repertoire, learn "Jazz Improvisation" solo along with the left hand voicings from Example 81. Continue on with a few solos of your own, applying all you know about improvisation.

Practical

_____ 1. Play "The Star Spangled Banner" by ear as in the Melodic Transposition Drill using both hands in all keys. Do this with several tunes of your choice.

_____ 2. Name, write out on staff paper, and play the chord scale that goes with the following chords: D7♭9(♭13), F♯m9, B♭°7, A7♯5(9), G13, B6(9), A♭m6(9), F7♯9, Gm7♭5, E7♭9.

_____ 3. Choose ten songs from any fake book—example: *The Real Book*, *The New Real Book*, etc., and convert the chords to advanced voicings per the chart in this lesson. Once converted, play the melody and **comp** with the advanced voicings. Suggested tunes to include are "Stella by Starlight," "Green Dolphin Street," "How High the Moon," "All the Things You Are," "Donna Lee," "All Blues," "A Night in Tunisia," "Giant Steps," "Sugar," "Footprints," "Goodbye Pork Pie Hat," "Night and Day," "On a Clear Day," and "Some Day My Prince Will Come."

_____ 4. Take each tune you learned in # 3 above, and practice soloing while you *comp* the voicings. Use notes from the four categories in the improvised line section: chord tones, passing tones, approach tones, and tensions (Example 43). Remember to practice your chord breakdowns as in Example 44 before you attempt outright soloing. Take your time—it takes as long as it takes!

Bonus Lesson
Lead Synth Techniques

Theory

Playing synth solos can be very liberating for the contemporary keyboardist as it a) allows him/her to experiment with different sounds other than piano. I used to always envy hearing guitarists bend notes and use their picking techniques to create interesting emotional effects. With the advent of the synthesizer, that has changed, but it does demand learning some new techniques, namely the *bending note* technique.

Bending Note Technique: The way this works conceptually is that one hears a certain note or chord that is bent either upwards or downwards a certain interval—a half step or whole step being the most common—and then plays a different note below or above in order to execute the bend. You have to get used to, in other words, playing the "wrong" note, and bending up to the "right" note. This simply takes some practice. Play the following drills and make sure you listen to the CD to really grasp how the bending works. As a side bar, synthesizers these days are pretty sophisticated with respect to the fact that programming capabilities include many, many parameters. Each sound can have different settings. I have some patches (sounds), for example, where I set the bend lever (wheel) range to only a whole step up or down to make playing half- and whole-step bends easier. However, this limits you because if you hear a minor third or octave bend, you're in trouble. So, there are two solutions: 1) Set the range to an octave and get used to the small bend movements to play half- and whole-step bends. This can be very tricky indeed. 2) Have the same sound stored with different bend ranges so you can easily switch back and forth. For more examples of great lead synth playing, listen to the works of the following artists: Chick Corea, George Duke, Jan Hammer, Keith Emerson, Herbie Hancock, and yours truly, John Novello with Niacin. There are, of course, many, many more, but these will get you started. I have included one of my synth solos from the Niacin CD entitled *Organik* as an example of lead synth playing.

While watching the music, listen to all of the following. "Combination Note Bending Etude" on page 88 uses all of the bend devices from Examples a–g.

Example 82: Note Bending

a) Half-Step Bends   d) Half-Step Trills/Tremolos   g) Minor Third Trills/Tremolos
b) Whole-Step Bends   e) Whole-Step Trills/Tremolos
c) Minor Third and Octave   f) Octave Trill

TRACK 83

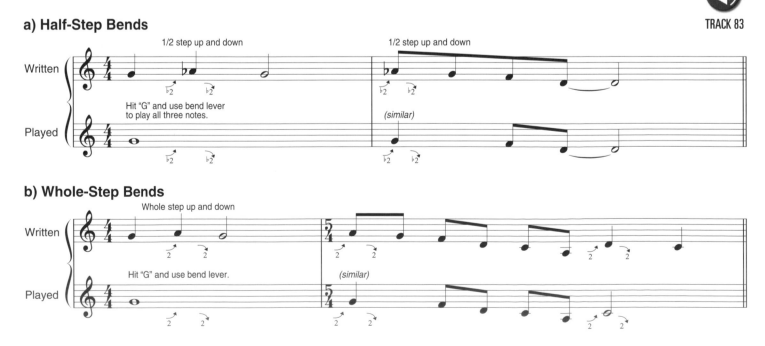

a) Half-Step Bends

b) Whole-Step Bends

86

c) Minor Third and Octave

d) Half-Step Trills/Tremolos

e) Whole-Step Trills/Tremolos

f) Octave Trill

g) Minor Third Trills/Tremolos

Combination Note Bending Etude

Note: Any bend can vary from slow to fast, meaning you can bend up to the desired note slowly or quickly. You should practice both, as they produce different amounts of tension.

"Hair of the Dog" from the Niacin CD *Organik*, Magnacarta Records © 2005. All Rights Reserved. Used by permission from **Niacin** featuring John Novello, keys; Billy Sheehan, bass; and Dennis Chambers, drums.

TRACK 84

Practical

_____ 1. Set your synth bend parameter to half step up or down, and practice playing any note, bending it up a half step, and back down. Next, do the same with a whole step.

_____ 2. Set your synth bend parameter to a minor third, and practice playing any note, then bending it up a minor third and back down.

_____ 3. Set your synth bend parameter to an octave, and then practice playing any note, then bending it up an octave and back down.

_____ 4. Learn the Combination Note Bending Etude, making sure you duplicate the exact bending patterns.

_____ 5. Listen to CD Track 81, "Hair of the Dog," making sure you identify each type of bend as you hear it. Do this with many lead synth solos from your favorite players.

Closing Remarks

Well, if you have honestly and successfully completed Lessons 1–13, then congratulations, as this was no easy task! You are no longer a beginner. You have trained your ear to hear basic intervals and to play what you hear. You have a beginning piano technique and dexterity, and a thorough understanding and use of basic chords and inversions. You have developed a good rhythmic feel and independence, and can improvise over chord changes. There is still much more to learn and experience, but, with this basic foundation to build on, you are on your way.

In order to continue your progress, I strongly suggest you study my other materials: *The Contemporary Keyboardist™, Stylistic Etudes,* and my three videos, *The Basics: Rhythm, Improv, and the Blues;* and *The Working Musician.* If you want to continue your studies, then I suggest you go to my website and register at CK online for private online instruction. These are private one-on-one instructions, directly with me. I also recommend you listen to a lot of music, both recorded and live, and study and extract as much as possible of what you like from these performances. And remember, there is no substitute for playing live and interacting with other musicians and, of course, with your audience. This is what it is all about. True musicianship simply translates into having something to say (passion from your heart) and then saying it as clearly and competently as possible. I can aid with the competence part by helping you learn your fundamentals, but *you* have to discover who you are and what you have to say. This is the challenge of life no matter what your gig. My advice is therefore to pursue the musical style(s) that *you* really like, for that is the path to your heart and the hearts of your audience. Play on!

Sincerely,

John Novello

Appendix

Appendix A: Major Scales

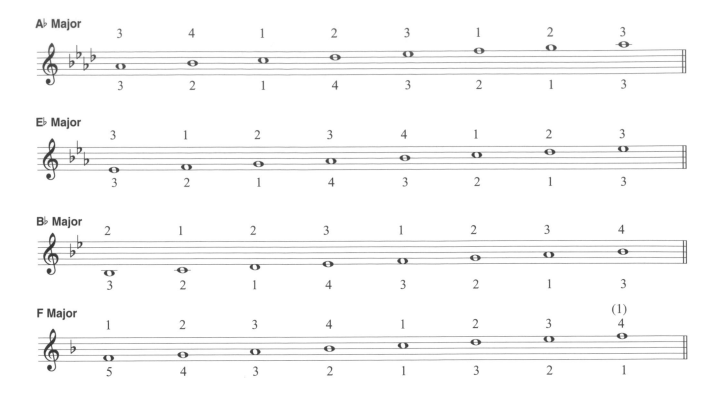

Appendix B: Minor Scales

There are more minor scales, but two of the most important for now are the harmonic minor (1, 2, ♭3, 4, 5, ♭6, 7, 1) and the melodic minor ascending or jazz minor as it's sometimes referred to (1, 2, ♭3, 4, 5, 6, 7, 1).

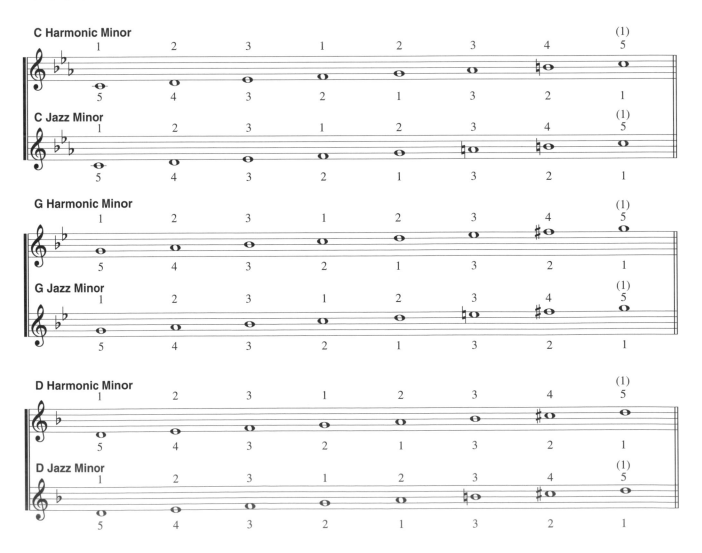

A Harmonic Minor

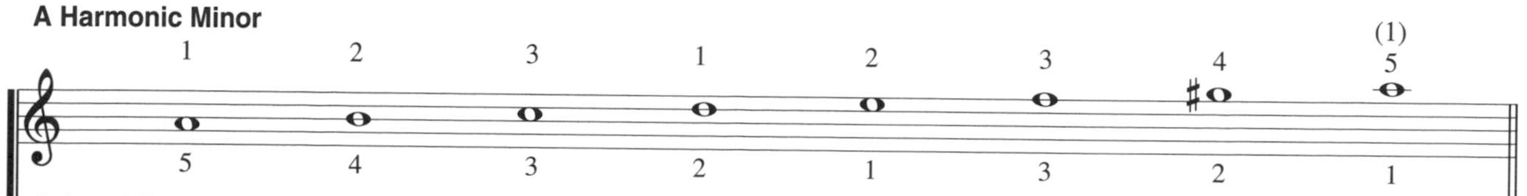

A Jazz Minor

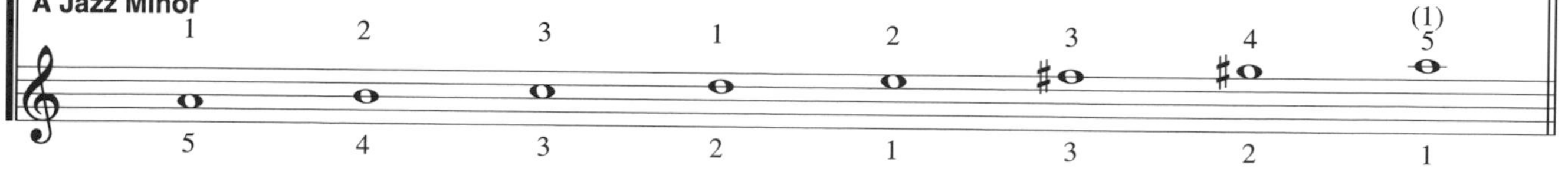

E Harmonic Minor

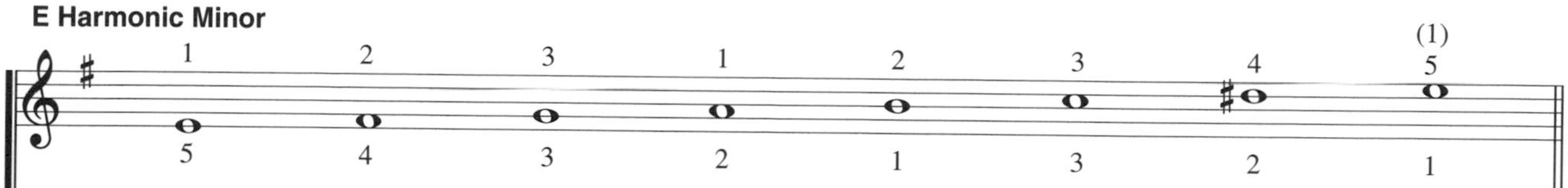

E Jazz Minor

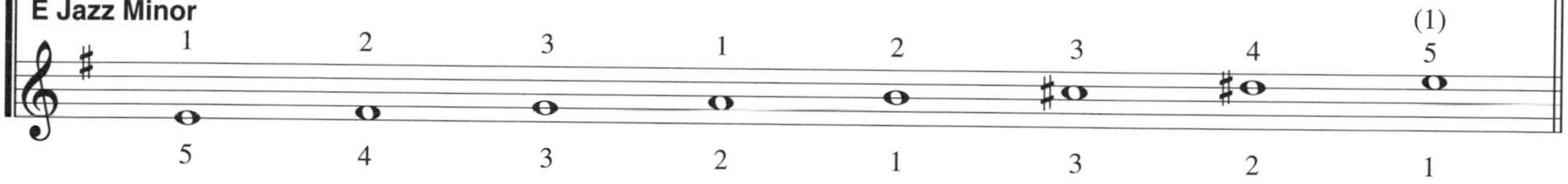

B Harmonic Minor

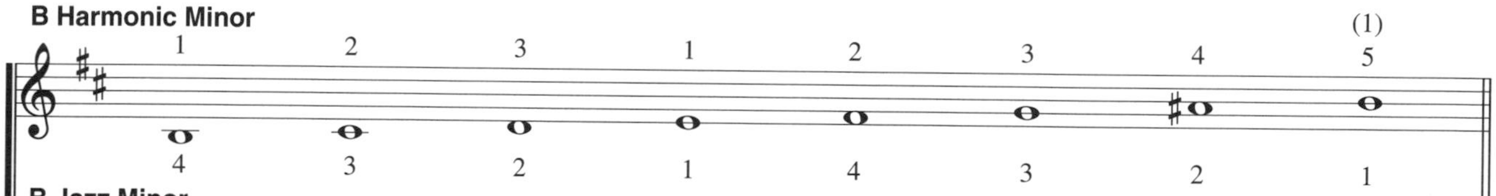

B Jazz Minor

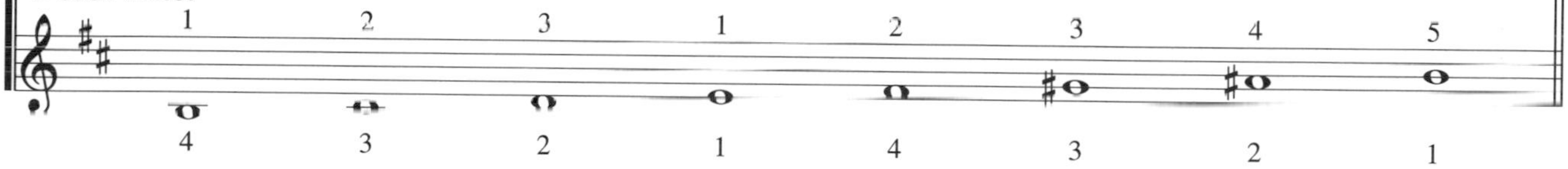

F♯ Harmonic Minor

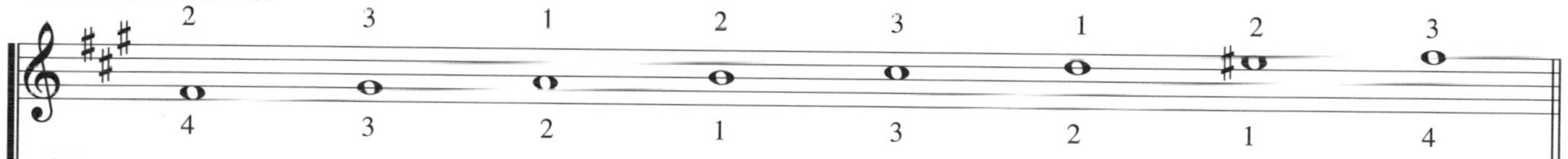

F♯ Jazz Minor

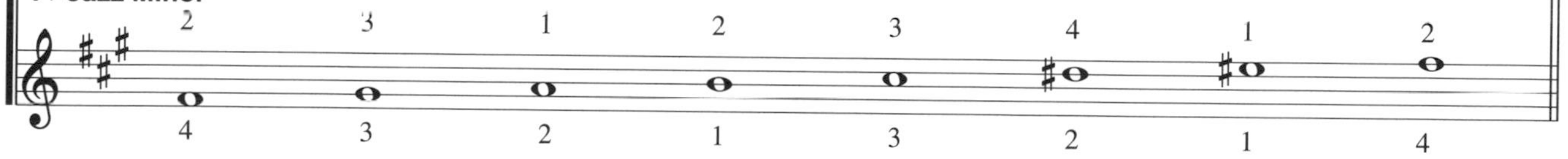

C♯ Harmonic Minor

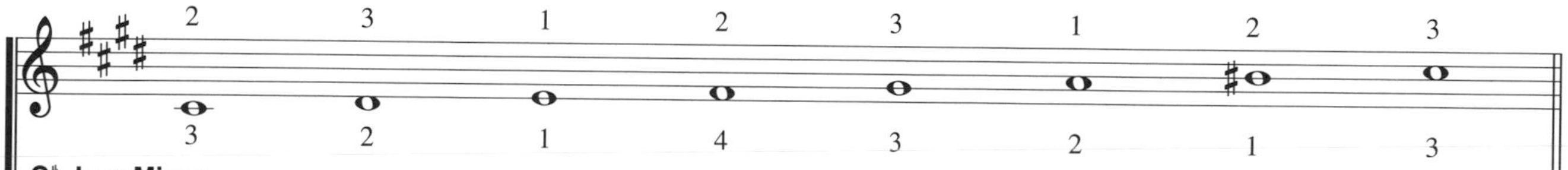

C♯ Jazz Minor

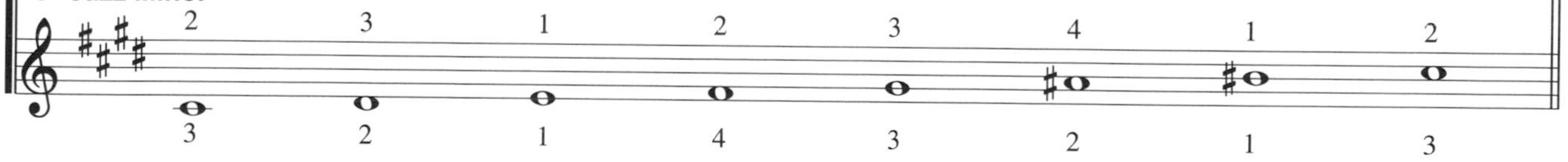

Ab Harmonic Minor

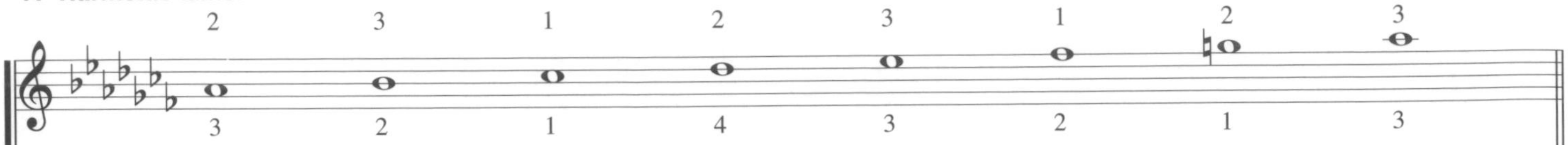

Ab Jazz Minor

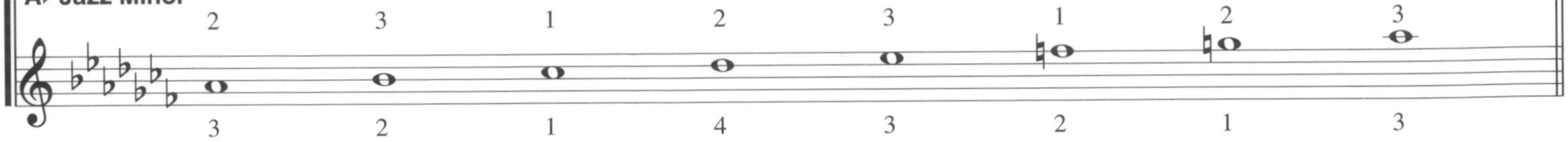

G# Harmonic Minor

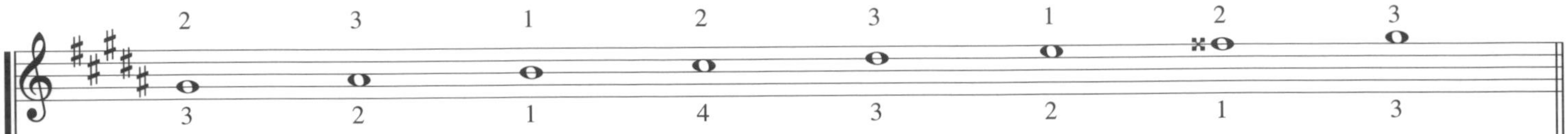

G# Jazz Minor

Eb Harmonic Minor

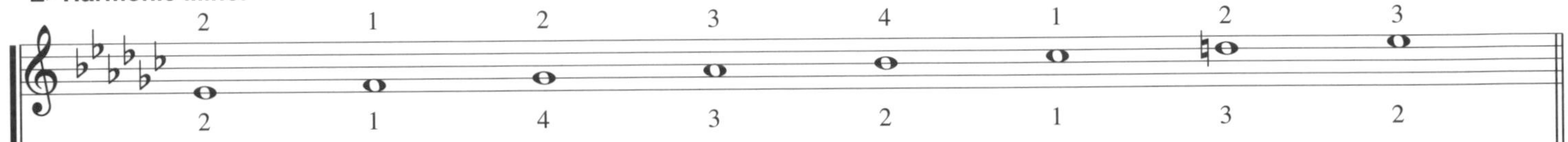

Eb Jazz Minor

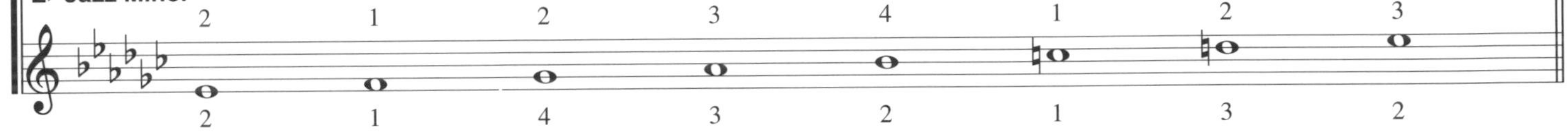

D# Harmonic Minor

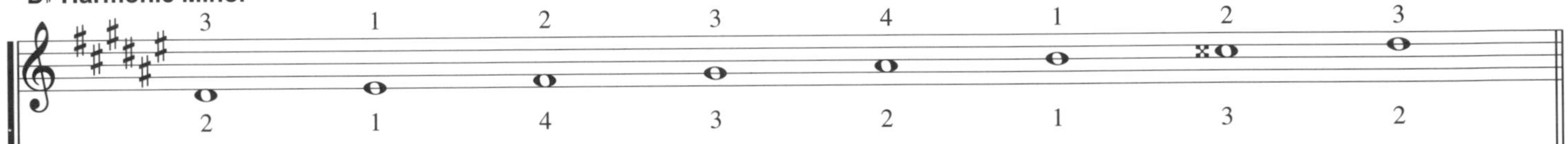

D# Jazz Minor

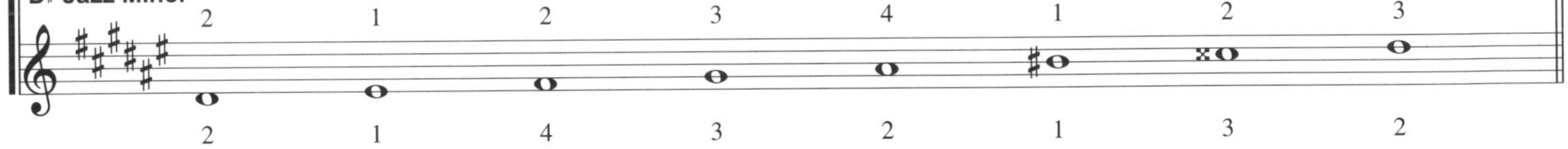

Bb Harmonic Minor

Bb Jazz Minor

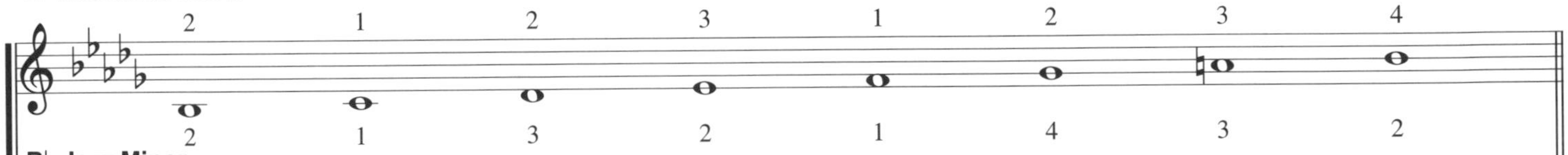

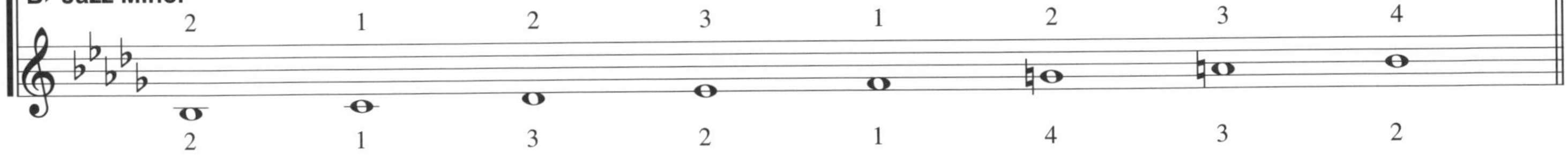

F Harmonic Minor

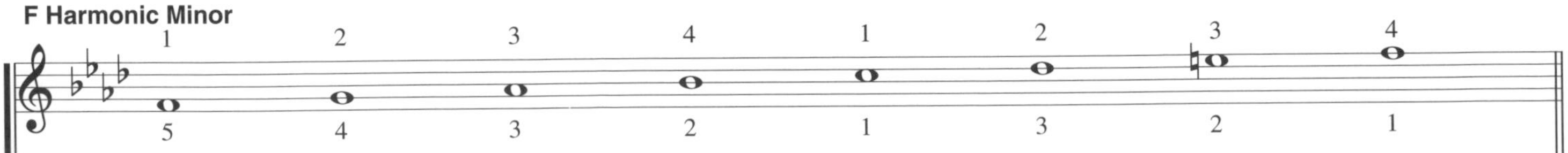

F Jazz Minor

Appendix C: The 19 Fundamental Chord Chart

The following chart is a complete list of all basic chord families (triads and tetrads). The chart shows the names, chord note formulas, and various chord symbols used. There are 19 chords and 12 keys or 228 fundamental chords that a contemporary keyboardist should know and be able to use in the major-minor tonal system. The example is in the key of C for ease of reference, but, of course, applies to all keys.

Chord Name	Chord Tone	Chord Symbols
Major triad	I, 3, 5	C, Cmaj, CM, Cma
Minor triad	I, ♭3, 5	Cm, Cmi, Cmin, C−
Diminished triad	I, ♭3, ♭5	C°, Cdim
Augmented triad	I, 3, ♯5	C+, Caug, C+5
Suspended 4 triad	I, 4, 5	Csus, Csus4
Suspended 2 triad	I, 2, 5	Csus2
Major 7	I, 3, 5, 7	Cmaj7, CM7, Cma7, C△, Cma7♯5
Major 7♯5	I, 3, ♯5, 7	Cmaj7+5, Cma7+5, C△+5
Major 7♭5	I, 3, ♭5, 7	Cmaj7♭5, Cma7♭5, C△♭5
Major 6	I, 3, 5, 6	C6, Cmaj6, CM6, Cma6
Minor major 7	I, ♭3, 5, 7	Cm(maj7), C−maj7, Cmin(maj7)
Minor 6	I, ♭3, 5, 6	Cm6, C−6, Cmin6, Cmi6
Minor 7	I, ♭3, 5, ♭7	Cm7, C−7, Cmi7, Cmin7
Minor 7♭5 (half diminished)	I, ♭3, ♭5, ♭7	Cm7♭5, Cmin7♭5, Cø, C−7♭5
Diminished 7	I, ♭3, ♭5, ♭♭7	C°7, Cdim7
Dominant 7	I, 3, 5, ♭7	C7, Cdom7
Augmented 7	I, 3, ♯5, 7	Caug7, C+7, C7+5, C7♯5
Dominant 7 suspended 4	I, 4, 5, ♭7	C7sus4, C7sus
Dominant 7♭5	I, 3, ♭5, ♭7	C7♭5

The 19 Fundamental Chord System

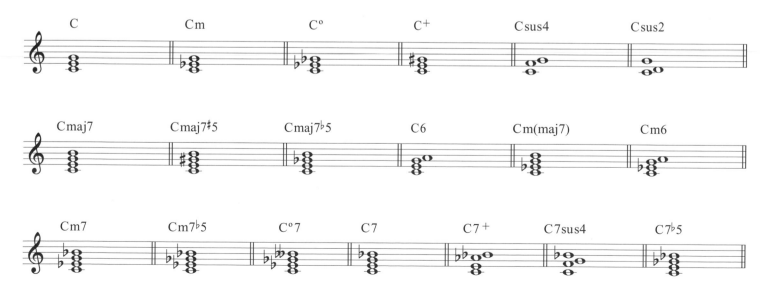

Appendix D: Tips for Success!

To use a computer analogy: If the software is bugged, doesn't matter how good the hardware is! That said, below is a software program (tips or successful actions), that if applied to your musical career (hardware: spirit, mind, and body), might keep you on the straight and narrow bridge to success.

0. Always operate on postulates and always postulate the ideal scene. This means whatever you want to achieve, imagine it as already done and achieved in *your* universe until it is actually done in the *physical* universe.

1. Make sure you're on purpose as an artist, meaning you're not in treason. Passion is everything, and if one is not doing exactly what they want (treason to yourself more or less), how can you expect to have any passion? Audiences aren't stupid; they know sincerity and passion. For example: if your hat and passion is progressive jazz fusion, then that's what you do, and promote up the conditions no matter what anybody else says or what the industry says. Never consult with anyone regarding your purpose other than yourself! And anybody or anything that gets in your way is politely ignored and/or removed as the case may warrant. Once you achieve what you wanted in an area, keep doing those things that got you there and/or move on to a new game or area.

2. Be very product and service oriented, meaning, to finish to professional competitive industry standards all products: CDs, videos, DVDs, music instruction manuals, performances, etc. The key thing here is finish so it can be released and exchanged with the public. A CD idea in one's head is not a valuable final product. You must confront the time and money and production barriers and finish the bloody thing! Waiting for that illusive record deal is totally being a victim. Wait for no one and depend on no one! Professional industry standards mean "how does it stand up to the standard that's currently selling or has been exchanged in the past?" One has to be brutally honest here, doesn't one? If one is a singer and sings a little out of tune, then one handles this; if one is a drummer and one's time is weak, well, get it handled. Promoting a weak product and/or service doesn't work. When and if it does, it eventually fails anyway, and besides, pride and accomplishment and work ethic apply here—that's what a pro is.

3. Always try and make your products and services in your area a knock-out so they produce an incredible effect on your public, and thus get great word of mouth. So, first it has to get past your professional standards, which you should postulate to be very high; then it has to get past your current evaluation of the industry's standards, which should be less than your own standards which is good, because if it's the other way around, you are dead! In other words, always try and go that extra mile and give way more than what might be expected.

4. Do lots of personal research in order to develop the correct business relationships with whom to promote your products and services. Some people call this "networking," but I hate that word as that usually relates to smoozing, which I don't really do (it's kind of pretentious, etc.). Personal research means contacting those who might be able to help in some way, surfing the internet, reading the trade magazines, going to concerts/clubs, and jamming with others. In other words, pay attention to your particular zone. Hoping someone will contact you doesn't work. You must flow inordinate amounts of energy outwards for that to occur. Also, you must do it because you want to... not only for the money and/or fame. That's why number one above is so, so important.

5. There should be no such thing in your universe as giving up! Just keep on out-flowing your products and services to the researched and developed relationships until your tea kettle whistles. If it doesn't whistle, never let it affect you for very long. Simply get even more determined and refine your products and services even further until it does.

6. Always keep in communication with your developed personal and business relationships, and flow them back the energy they flowed you when they need it. This includes your fans!!!

Glossary

This glossary of terms contains not only key technical terms, but also non-technical ones that sometimes get in the way of understanding. Terms that are sufficiently defined already in the main text are not included in this glossary. Once you look up a word you don't fully grasp, always use it in a few sentences until you really own it. This is extremely important for correct duplication, understanding, and application.

Accidental

Also called an "inflection," sign, for raising (using a sharp or double sharp) or lowering (using a flat or double flat) the pitch of a note or for canceling (using a natural) a previously applied sign.

Avant-Garde

An intelligentsia new or experimental concepts, especially in the arts.

Baroque Period

The musical period approximately between 1600 and 1750 encompassing composers such as Monteverdi, Frescobaldi and Gabrieli (early baroque), and Bach and Handel (late baroque). It is characterized by elaborate treatment of melody in polyphonic style.

Bebop

Also referred to as "Bop," this is 1) an early form of modern jazz (originating around 1940), 2) jazz characterized by harmonic complexity, convoluted melodic lines, and constant shifting of accents, often played at very rapid tempos, 3) the music of Charlie Parker, known as "Bird."

Body

1) The material part or nature of a human being; 2) the physical bio-unit that is used by a spirit to play the game of life.

Blues

A style of music evolved from Southern African-American secular songs and usually distinguished by a syncopated 4/4 rhythm. Blues includes the use of flatted thirds and sevenths, a 12-bar structure, and lyrics in a three-line stanza in which the second line repeats the first: "The blues is an expression of anger against shame and humiliation." (B.B. King)

Classical

1) Of or relating to European music during the latter half of the 18th and the early 19th centuries; 2) of or relating to music in the educated European tradition, such as symphony and opera, as opposed to popular or folk music.

Classical Period

A period in the late 18th century when composers such as Haydn and Mozart wrote music characterized by clarity of texture, harmony and melody, as well as the refinement of abstract musical forms such as the sonata, symphony and concerto.

Clef

The symbol used to determine the relative position of notes on the musical staff, placed normally at the beginning of each line, or whenever a different clef temporarily replaces the starting clef (to make notes fit more easily on the staff). There are many possible clefs (for example, treble, bass, alto, and tenor) chosen to accommodate the range of various instruments or voices. In piano music, the grand staff (a staff for each hand) uses treble and bass clefs.

Comp

An abridged or slang term for accompaniment. In piano playing, this refers to the harmonic and rhythmic accompaniment a pianist uses to accompany or support a melody whether played by himself or another musician. Chick Corea, for example, is considered to be a great "comper."

Contemporary

1) Happening, existing, living, or coming into being during the same period of time, 2a) simultaneous, 2b) marked by characteristics of the present period: modern or current.

Country Music

Music derived from or imitating the folk style of the Southern U.S.

Diatonic

Of or relating to notes that occur naturally in a scale, without being modified by accidentals other than in the key signature.

Digital

1) Of or relating to the fingers or toes; 2) done with a finger; 3) of, relating to, or using calculation by numerical methods or by discrete units; 4) of or relating to data in the form of numerical digits, 5) providing a readout in numerical digits (a *digital* voltmeter), 6) characterized by electronic and computerized technology (living in a *digital* world), 7) relating to an audio recording method in which sound waves are represented digitally (as on magnetic tape) so that in the recording wow and flutter are eliminated and background noise is reduced.

Disklavier

An acoustic piano that can play itself using previously recorded disks (CDs), the Disklavier can also capture a performer's actions as digital data and play such data back "live" with an exceptional degree of fidelity and nuance.

Fundamental

1a) Serving as an original or generating source; 1b) serving as a basis supporting existence or determining essential structure or function, BASIC; 2a) of or relating to essential structure, function, or facts also: of or dealing with general principles rather than practical application, (*fundamental* science); 2b) adhering to fundamentalism; 3) of, relating to, or produced by the lowest component of a complex vibration; 4) of central importance: PRINCIPAL (*fundamental* purpose), 5) belonging to ones innate or ingrained characteristics: DEEP-ROOTED (her **fundamental** good humor); synonym: see "essential."

Funk

A distinct style of music originated by African-Americans, i.e., James Brown and his band members (especially Maceo and Melvin Parker) and groups like The Meters. Funk best can be recognized by its syncopated rhythms and 16th-note feel; thick bass line (often based on an "on the one" beat); razor-sharp rhythm guitars; chanted or hollered vocals (as that of Marva Whitney or the Bar-Kays); strong, rhythm-oriented horn sections as in Tower of Power, Sly and The Family Stone, Earth Wind and Fire; prominent percussion; an upbeat attitude; African tones; danceability; and strong jazz influences (i.e., the music of Miles Davis, Herbie Hancock, George Duke, Eddie Harris, and others).

Fusion/Jazz Fusion

Sometimes referred to simply as "fusion," this is a musical genre that loosely encompasses the merging of jazz with other styles, particularly rock, funk, R&B, and world music. It basically involved jazz musicians mixing the forms and techniques of jazz with the electric instruments of rock, and rhythmic structure from African-American popular music, both "soul" and "rhythm and blues." The 1970s were the most important decade for fusion, but the style has been well represented during later decades. Fusion albums, often even those that are made by the same artist, include a variety of musical styles. It can be argued that rather than being a coherent musical style, fusion is a musical tradition and approach.

Glib

Showing little forethought or preparation; lacking depth and substance; superficial.

Hardware

1) ware (as fittings, cutlery, tools, utensils, or parts of machines) made of metal; 2) major items of equipment or their components for a particular purpose, the physical components (as electronic and electrical devices) of a vehicle (as a spacecraft) or an apparatus (as a computer).

Harmony

This is the use and study of pitch simultaneity and chords, actual or implied, in music. It is sometimes referred to as the "vertical" aspect of music, with melody being the "horizontal" aspect. Very often, harmony is a result of counterpoint or polyphony, several melodic lines or motifs being played at once, though harmony may control the counterpoint. The word *harmony* comes from the Greek ἁρμονία *harmonía*, meaning "a fastening or join." The concept of harmony dates as far back as Pythagoras.

Inner Soul

You, the spiritual being in charge of your mind and body, of your dreams and goals, sometimes referred to as your "higher self."

Jam

A jam session is a musical act where musicians gather and play (or "jam"). The word "jam" can be more loosely used to refer to any particularly inspired or improvisational part of a musical performance, especially in rock and jazz music.

Jazz

A musical art form originally developed by African-Americans around the turn of the 20th century. It is characterized by blue notes, syncopation, swing, call and response, polyrhythms, and improvisation. As the first original art form to emerge from the United States of America, jazz has been described as "America's Classical Music." Jazz has roots in the cultural and musical expression of West Africa and the western Sahel, and in African-American music traditions, including blues and ragtime, as well as European military band music. After originating in African-American communities near the beginning of the 20th century, jazz gained international popularity by the 1920s. Since then, jazz has had a profoundly pervasive influence on other musical styles worldwide. Today, various jazz styles continue to evolve.

Licks

Short catchy musical phrases or themes created by musicians and handed down. A player usually in the process of learning how to improvise may copy the licks of many of his mentors in order to better understand the music. In the end, the goal is to be able to make those licks your own and thus create your own licks or phrases.

McCoy

Something that is neither imitation or substitute: often used in the phrase "the real McCoy."

Metronome

A device that produces a regular pulse, usually used to keep a steady beat in musical rehearsal.

MIDI

Musical Instrument Digital Interface is an industry-standard electronic communication protocol that defines each musical note in an electronic musical instrument such as a synthesizer, precisely and concisely, allowing electronic musical instruments and computers to exchange data, or "talk" with each other. MIDI does not transmit audio—it simply transmits digital information about a music performance.

Mind

The organized conscious and unconscious adaptive mental activity of an organism.

Motif / Motive

A short tune or musical figure that characterizes and unifies a composition. It can be of any length, but is usually only a few notes long. A motif can be a melodic, harmonic, or rhythmic pattern that is easily recognizable throughout the composition.

Music

This is a natural intuitive phenomenon operating in the three worlds of time, pitch, and energy, and under the three distinct and interrelated organization structures of rhythm, harmony, and melody.

Opus

A term used to classify a composition in relation to the composer's other compositions. Abbreviated as "Op." (work) or "Opp." (works), compositions are typically given an opus number in chronological order (i.e., "Op. 1," "Op. 2," etc.). Because the opus numbers are often assigned by publishers, they are not always a reliable indication of the chronology of the composition.

Orientation

The act or process of being intellectually, emotionally, or functionally directed.

Permutation(s)

A complete change; a transformation. The act of altering a given set of objects in a group. In mathematics, this consists of a rearrangement of the elements of a set.

Phrase

A series of notes that display a complete musical sense form a natural division of the melodic line, comparable to a phrase in discourse, and constituting a complete whole (a melodic phrase subdivides into various parts that correspond to the indices of discourse).

Pocket

In music, this refers to the overall time and the subdivisions that a player demonstrates in his/her performance; basically, it's the groove!

Pop

Depending on context, pop music is either an abbreviation of popular music or, more recently, a term for a sub genre of it. In general, pop music features simple, memorable melodies with catchy, sing-along choruses. Pop songs often have a hook, one or more musical ideas repeated to "hook" a listener's interest. A hook can be any part of the song: musical, rhythmic, vocal, or as is most often the case, a mixture of all of them. Pop music is usually instantly accessible to anyone who is culturally inclined to take part, even the musical novice.

Practical

A drill and/or an assignment designed to supplement theoretical training by hands-on experience.

Prerequisite(s)

Something that is necessary to an end or to the carrying out of a function.

Random

A haphazard course, at random, without definite aim, direction, rule, or method.

Renaissance

1) *Capitalized;* 1a) the transitional movement in Europe between medieval and modern times beginning in the 14th century in Italy, lasting into the 17th century, and marked by a humanistic revival of classical influence expressed in a flowering of the arts and literature and by the beginnings of modern science; 1b) the period of the Renaissance; 1c) the neoclassic style of architecture prevailing during the Renaissance; 2) *often capitalized:* a movement or period of vigorous artistic and intellectual activity; 3) rebirth or revival.

Rock

Rock and roll (also spelled "rock 'n' roll," especially in its first decade) is a genre of music that emerged as a defined musical style in America in the 1950s. It later evolved into the various different subgenres of what is now called simply "rock." Early rock and roll combined elements of blues, boogie woogie, jazz, and rhythm and blues.

Romantic Period

The era of Romantic music is defined as the period of European classical music that runs roughly from the early 1800s to the first decade of the 20th century, as well as music written according to the norms and styles of that period. The Romantic period was preceded by the Classical period, and was followed by the modern period. The Romanticism movement held that not all truth could be deduced from axioms, that there were inescapable realities in the world which could only be reached through emotion, feeling, and intuition.

Scat

Scat singing consists of vocalizing either wordlessly, or with nonsense, words and syllables as employed by jazz singers who create the equivalent of an instrumental solo using only the voice. Thus, it is a type of voice instrumental.

Software

Computer software is essentially a computer program encoded in such a fashion that the program (the instruction set) contents can be changed with minimal effort. Computer software can have various functions such as controlling hardware, performing computations, communication with other software, human interaction, etc., all of which are prescribed in the program. The term "software" was first used in this sense by John W. Tukey in 1957. Computer science and software engineering is all information processed by computer system, programs, and data. The concept of software was first proposed by Alan Turing in an essay.

Soloing

In music, "solo" means to play or sing alone. This does not necessarily mean that no one else is playing at that time, only that the soloist's part is the most prominent. Solos are a chance for a musician to show off his or her musicianship, which often includes speed and technique. In improvised solos, a musician also demonstrates his/her creativity. In jazz, solos are usually improvised. It is common for two or more musicians to improvise together, trading ideas as they alternate playing—a musical conversation of sorts.

Spirit

The spirit or soul, according to many religious and philosophical traditions, is the ethereal substance particular to a unique living being. Such traditions often consider the soul both immortal and innately aware of its immortal nature, as well as the true basis for sentience in each living being, the being itself as separate from the body and the mind—YOU!

Stylistic

Of or pertaining to a musical genre (type) in reference to music. For example: jazz, blues, rock, gospel, classical, etc.

Synthesizer

A synthesizer is an electronic musical instrument designed to produce electronically generated sound, using techniques such as additive, subtractive, FM, physical modeling synthesis, or phase distortion. Synthesizers create sounds through direct manipulation of electrical voltages (as in analog synthesizers), mathematical manipulation of discrete values using computers (as in software synthesizers), or by a combination of both methods

Theory

The general or abstract principles of a body of fact, a science, or an art (music theory)—the branch of a science or art consisting of its explanatory statements, accepted principles, and methods of analysis, as opposed to practice: a fine musician who had never studied theory.

Tonic

The note upon which a scale or key is based; the first note of a scale or key; the keynote; the key center; in reference to harmony, the I chord which indicates static or at rest as compared to the Dominant or V chord which is tense and moving.

Topography

1) The configuration of a surface, including its relief and the position of its natural and man-made features; 2) the physical or natural features of an object or entity and their structural relationships.

Treason

The betrayal of a trust. (Note: one can be in treason or treasonous to himself; for example, by not being true to his purpose.)

Trill

An ornament that consists of rapid alternation between one tone and another tone, either a step or a semitone away from the first tone.

Universe

The whole body of things and phenomena observed or postulated; a distinct field or province of thought or reality that forms a closed system or self-inclusive and independent organization; a set that contains all elements relevant to a particular discussion or problem.

Index